"This book is excellent. I read a
service to those of us who are tea......
congratulations to the autho ..."

Claire Carroll, SSJ
St. Joseph University
Philadelphia, Pennsylvania

"In this congenial book R. Rhys Williams introduces general readers of the Bible to some basic principles of modern gospel research. Readers are addressed personally, as "you," and led without condescension through methods of interpretation that allow each of the four canonical gospels to express its own uniqueness and integrity. The result is that one begins to see the evangelists more as artists than as newspaper reporters. Yet the faithfulness of their witness is in no way diminished. Indeed, the richness of their words about Jesus comes again and again to the surface. Each gospel becomes more interesting in its own right, and so their combined message emerges as something more and better than the simple harmony many of us were taught as children or young adults. Williams has written a lively guide to the gospels by means of which contemporary laypeople and clergy can teach one another."

John Koenig
Professor of New Testament
The General Theological Seminary
New York, New York

"Williams's book is a good introduction to Redaction Criticism of the gospels for anybody who knows little or nothing about the scholarly approach to Scripture. His notes are particularly useful in this regard. I hope it will be widely used."

Dr. J.C. Kirby
Atlantic School of Theology
Halifax, Nova Scotia

"Williams shows himself to be a master teacher in the inductive way in which he presents his material. First he gives an expository presentation of redaction criticism, but does so by letting the interpretation emerge from the reader's study of the texts rather than by stating theories that the reader somehow has to relate to the texts. Then he provides a glossary as a first level of follow-up reading. Next come notes that explain things too complicated for the body of the book. The notes include exercises so that the reader can develop personal skills as an interpreter of the gospels. And finally there is a good list of reading by which the neophyte exegete can move on from this initiation. An excellent introductory work for either personal study or class use."

Rev. O.C. Edwards, Jr.
Seabury Western Theological Seminary
Evanston, Illinois

"Dr. Williams's skill in describing and then demonstrating scholarly approaches to the study of the gospels gives promise that *Let Each Gospel Speak for Itself* will be a useful, stimulating tool for lay study in the churches. While avoiding scholarly jargon, he introduces to the reader an admirable array of interpretive insights and issues in direct, candid style. By starting out with those parts of the gospel tradition that are best known to the average church-goer — Christmas and Easter stories — he shows how essential this kind of analytical study is for understanding the gospels on their own terms. The selective bibliography and the perceptive study notes further enhance the value of this book, which should make a major contribution to the student and adult generation of seeking lay Christians. And it is likely that some clergy will pick up some important insights, as well!"

Howard C. Kee
William Goodwin Aurelio
Professor of Biblical Studies
Boston University
Boston, Massachusetts

This volume deliberately pits one gospel against another so as to let the unique message of each reveal itself. Thus is the reader immersed from the start in one of the major methodical breakthroughs in recent New Testament study, namely, redaction criticism.

Williams's approach is both ingenious and absorbing. He begins with the Christmas story—in the Gospels of Matthew and Luke, of course, but then also more surprisingly in Mark and John. His typically sensitive attention to the reader's faith is evident: he follows the way the church, over the centuries and still now, uses each of the four gospels in the context of the feast of Christ's coming into the world. This, then, is no conventional focus simply on the birth of Jesus.

Similarly the Easter and Good Friday stories are in turn exposed in their four expressions. Finally, the reader is introduced to the four gospels as wholes and brought to the task, by means of skillfully conceived study notes, of using the text itself, in order to pose and answer the questions the text demands be addressed. We have, in short, a manual for a first-hand study of the gospels.

This book is altogether rich in potential for the reader, demanding in its expectations, and novel in its approach. In the end, it is both highly engaging and inspiring.

Robert T. Fortna
Professor of Religion
Vassar College
Poughkeepsie, New York

To my mother and father
who taught me to read the Bible.
Nihil Longe Deo!

LET EACH GOSPEL SPEAK FOR ITSELF

R. RHYS WILLIAMS

TWENTY-THIRD PUBLICATIONS
Mystic, Connecticut

Acknowledgments

The Scripture quotations contained herein are from the Revised Standard Version of the Bible, copyrighted 1946, 1952, 1971, by the Division of Christian Education of the National Council of the Churches of Christ in the USA, and are used by permission. All rights reserved.

The quotations from *The Nag Hammadi Library in English* (Logions 63, 97, and 98) by James M. Robinson, editor, are reprinted by permission of Harper & Row (San Francisco, 1977).

About the cover

The cover photos taken in Saint Agnes Cathedral in Rockville Centre, New York, are the traditional symbols connected with the evangelists. These depict easily identifiable ways to distinguish each gospel story as unique.

Matthew's angel signifies the messengers from God that characterize the infancy narratives of the first gospel.

Mark's king of the desert, the lion, recalls the opening of the second gospel with John the Baptist in the desert.

Luke's sacrificial oxen brings to mind the beginning of the third gospel with Zechariah offering sacrifice to God in the temple.

John's eagle calls attention to the soaring theology and the high christology of the fourth gospel.

**Twenty-Third Publications
P.O. Box 180
Mystic, CT 06355
(203) 536-2611**

© 1987 R. Rhys Williams. All rights reserved. No part of this publication may be reproduced in any manner, except for brief excerpts in critical reviews, without prior written permission of the publisher. Write to Permissions Editor.

ISBN 0-89622-327-2
Library of Congress Catalog Card Number 86-51537

Cover photo by Thomas Moloney
Cover design by Bill Baker
Edited by Walter Nott
Designed by John G. van Bemmel

Contents

Introduction   1

Chapter 1   The Christmas Stories   7
Matthew's Christmas Story   7
Luke's Christmas Story   15
John's Christmas Story   21
Mark's Christmas Story   25

Chapter 2   The Easter Stories   29
Mark's Easter Story   32
Matthew's Easter Story   35
Luke's Easter Story   38
John's Easter Story   42

Chapter 3   The Good Friday Stories   47
Mark's Good Friday Story   48
Matthew's Good Friday Story   52
Luke's Good Friday Story   54
John's Good Friday Story   57

Chapter 4   The Gospels   63
Mark's Story of the Good News of Jesus   65
Matthew's Story of the Good News of Jesus   70
Luke's Story of the Good News of Jesus   74
John's Story of the Good News of Jesus   79

Conclusion 85

Study Notes 89
    For the Introduction   90
    For Chapter 1   94
    For Chapter 2   98
    For Chapter 3   104
    For Chapter 4   110
    For Conclusion   121

Suggestions for Further Reading 122

Glossary 125

Introduction

This book is intended to help you learn to let each gospel speak for itself. It is not another explanation of the meaning of the gospels but an introduction to a different method of studying the gospels.

The approach proposed in this book takes the creative function of the gospel writer seriously. An evangelist is like a composer who brings together several components to produce a new piece of music. Think, for example, of the way Tchaikovsky weaves various folk melodies into his distinctive creations and you will have a notion of what we are talking about when we describe the work of an evangelist.

This approach considers each gospel a unique composition of traditional material proclaiming Jesus as the Christ. Each gospel was composed for a particular community, and the message it proclaims has a special relevance for that congregation.

Such an approach is not new. Scholars pioneered in applying this method of studying the Bible to the gospels in the late 1950s.[1] So far, however, this approach has not had much impact on the average, serious student of the New Testament or on the parish clergy. It is probably new to you.

Try the following experiment to demonstrate this to yourself. Take a piece of paper and, without consulting your

Bible, list briefly the incidents in the Christmas story. Do it from memory as rapidly as you can, without reflection.

Now examine your list. Most likely it includes the annunciation to Mary of the birth of Jesus, preceded possibly by the annunciation of the birth of John the Baptist; the visitation by Mary to Elizabeth; the birth of Jesus, laid in a manager in Bethlehem; the visit of the shepherds, who hear the good news from angels; the visit of the Wise Men, led by a star; the flight of the Holy Family to Egypt, plus possibly the slaughter of the innocent boys in Bethlehem; and the family's return to Nazareth after the death of Herod the Great. You may also have sandwiched in somewhere the presentation of the infant Jesus in the temple in Jerusalem and, if you are very knowledgeable, you may have listed the genealogy of Jesus.

Such a list is not surprising since most of us were brought up on a harmonized version of the Christmas story which combines portions of the birth narratives of Matthew and Luke. This is the basis of most Christmas pageants, and it is reflected in the traditional Christmas crèche.

A more careful consideration of the Christmas story, however, shows which incidents came from Luke's birth narrative and which from Matthew's. This is obvious to you, *once it has been pointed out*. But, unless you are exceptional, this did not occur to you as you were listing the incidents in the Christmas story. Then you thought of it as a single story made up of all these events which were somehow connected. Taken separately, each birth narrative tells a different story.

Further examination of the four gospels reveals that the gospel of Mark and the gospel of John do not tell a birth story at all. There is no single Christmas story in the gospels. There are, indeed, *four* Christmas stories.

The purpose of this book is to help you shift from the traditional approach to the gospels, which harmonizes the material in them into a so-called life of Jesus, to a different approach which emphasizes the unique message of each gospel. So we shall consider each gospel separately, and we shall consider all four gospels, the Synoptic gospels — Matthew, Mark, and Luke (so-called because they take a common perspective) — plus John.

The book is designed to help you learn to read each gospel on different levels. On the first level, each gospel tells a story of a community that believes in Jesus. So we shall be concerned, primarily, with the particular way each evangelist presents Jesus to his community and, secondarily, with the pregospel history of the tradition used by the evangelist. In this way we shall come to realize that each gospel writer is a creative composer who arranged traditional material in his unique way for his particular purposes.

On the second level, each gospel offers limited means for reconstructing the ministry and message of Jesus. So we shall be interested in the way each evangelist, *by telling the story of Jesus in his own manner,* contributes to our knowledge of the life of Jesus.

We shall, of course, take full advantage of all the careful study of the separate segments of the gospels and their literary form[2] and the results of the extensive scholarship on the interrelationship of the Synoptic gospels and on the development of the Fourth Gospel.[3] But we shall take one further step. We shall look at each gospel separately, as a child of its time, and at each evangelist as a creative artist who combines traditional material into his own special composition.

The method employed in this book is simple. We shall ask the following questions of each of the gospel passages we study. First, what would I know about the story of Jesus if I had only this gospel account? This will involve isolating that particular gospel's account from the others and, then, comparing the same account in all the gospels to determine what is unique in the account being examined. Second, in what context does the evangelist place this account? Context is often the clue to the meaning the evangelist gives to the material he inherited from the tradition. Third, for what community is the evangelist writing his gospel? The answer to this question will often provide the key to the gospel writer's particular interest and purpose.

Take, for example, the Christmas story. What would you know of the beginning of Jesus' life if you possessed, say, only Luke's gospel? Remember that each gospel was produced for a particular congregation and had a separate existence to begin with. What then is unique about the way Luke tells the story of Jesus' birth? How does it differ from Matthew's version of the same tradition of the virgin birth of Jesus? How is Luke's account of the birth story of Jesus related to his gospel and to the Book of Acts? Does Matthew use his version of the birth story of Jesus for the same purpose as Luke does? What do the answers to these questions tell us about the community for which Luke composed his gospel?

The plan of the book is straightforward. We shall consider, first, the Christmas story in each of the four gospels. This is the easiest place to introduce the techniques of the approach taken in this book, and I have already tantalized you by involving you in the process of examining the birth stories from this different perspective.

Then we shall consider the Easter story in each of the gospels. For the early church, and for the evangelists, this was the beginning of the story of Jesus. Following that we shall examine the Good Friday story, the passion narrative, in each of the gospels. This was probably the earliest part of the story which was fixed by the tradition. So a study of this material will test our method.

By our examination of these three aspects of the story of Jesus, I hope to help you develop sufficient familiarity with this approach to biblical study and a reasonable facility with the techniques of this method so that you can begin to apply this different perspective in your own study of the gospels. The final chapter of the book, then, will be devoted to summarizing the results of our examination, identifying the techniques used in this method of study, and providing you with some directions for further study of each gospel.

In the conclusion we shall let the church speak for itself and explain briefly why these gospels were included in its canonical scriptures and why all four gospel accounts were needed to tell the church's story of Jesus.

For those of you who wish to pursue the study in more detail or more depth, Study Notes are appended. They include further information about specific topics, recommended reading, and questions for reflection and discussion. They will be particularly useful to Bible study groups, their leaders, and the clergy. The notes are arranged by chapter, and reference is made to them at appropriate places in the text.

A Glossary is also included to help you with the more difficult terms of this study.

You will find it necessary to read this book with your Bible at hand. It will be important for you to work through the biblical material presented in each section. Since you will often be asked to compare gospel versions of a passage, a parallel version of the gospels, at least of the Synoptics, will be helpful.[4] If such a tool is not available, try using several copies of the Bible, each opened to a different gospel account.

The approach proposed in this book will be of particular interest to those of you who belong to churches which employ a scheme of Sunday gospel readings which focuses, in turn, on one gospel a year. But it will be of use to all serious students of the Bible, lay and clergy alike, who seek a deeper understanding of the gospels.

The familiar approach to the gospels that harmonizes the material in them to form a single story of Jesus leads to a homogenized, hence bland and colorless, portrayal of the Christ. The approach proposed in this book, on the other hand, preserves the uniqueness of each gospel and provides us in the end with a fuller understanding of Jesus.

The gospels are like portraits in an exhibition. Each was "painted" in its own way and, originally, viewed separately. Now they hang side by side because the church felt all four were necessary to tell the story. By letting each "portrait" of Jesus speak for itself we shall preserve the richness of the gospel tradition. That is the aim of this book.

1

The Christmas Stories

Two of the Christmas stories are birth narratives — one in Matthew and the other in Luke — and they are quite different. We shall begin by isolating Matthew's version of the infancy story. Ask yourself, What would I know about Jesus' birth if I possessed only Matthew's gospel?

Matthew's Christmas Story

Read through the first two chapters of Matthew to refresh your memory and, for the moment, pretend you don't know anything about Luke's birth story. You will see that Matthew presents his account in four episodes. First, he gives the genealogy of Jesus (1:1-17). Then he tells about the conception of Jesus and his birth (1:18-25). Following that, he describes the visit of the Wise Men (2:1-12) and the flight of the Holy Family to Egypt and their return to Nazareth after the death of Herod the Great (2:13-23).

By isolating Matthew's birth story we are able to observe more clearly both what use he makes of traditional material and what unique material he introduces into his version of the infancy narrative. It is obvious that Matthew doesn't start from scratch to tell his Christmas story. He knows about the tradition that Jesus was born in Bethlehem and grew up in Nazareth. He is also aware of a tradition of what is usually called the virgin birth but is more precisely the virginal conception of Jesus.[1] The fact that Luke also knew of these traditions is evidence that they had some currency in the early church.

Matthew also employs traditional material, not found elsewhere, which is composed of dream sequences in which God's will and word are made known. Look up the following passages in which important messages from God are imparted: 1:20,24, where God speaks to Joseph in a dream to tell him about the conception of Jesus and commands him to take Mary as his wife; 2:12, where God warns the Wise Men in a dream not to return to Herod; 2:13, where God warns Joseph in a dream to take his family and flee to Egypt; and 2:19-20, where "an angel of the Lord" appears in a dream to tell Joseph to take the child and his mother back to Israel.

More interesting to us, however, are the unique features of Matthew's birth story. Matthew makes Joseph the chief actor in his account. In his version of the story, Mary and Joseph live in Bethlehem. They do not come from Galilee. They have no problem finding a room in the inn. Joseph has a house in Bethlehem to which he takes Mary when she is betrothed to him. He marries Mary as the Lord commands him in a dream, and when the child is born he names him, thus establishing his legal paternity.

Matthew also emphasizes the role played by Herod the Great. The Wise Men visit Herod asking for the new king, and because of Herod's jealous wrath Joseph is forced to take his family to Egypt where they remain until the death of Herod. Only then do they dare return to their native land, but prudently they decide to settle in Nazareth.

With these general observations in mind let us examine this material more closely. Take note, in particular, of a stylistic peculiarity of Matthew, namely, his use of formula citations. Matthew 1:22-23 is a good example of this. The key phrase is, "All this took place to fulfill what the Lord had spoken by the prophet." This is followed by a quotation from the Old Testament, the scriptures of both Jews and early Christians. In this case it is from Isaiah 7:14.

The theme that actions and events in the story of Jesus are the fulfillment of the law and the prophets is characteristic of Matthew's gospel. There are fourteen formula citations in Matthew, five of which are in these first two chapters. There is only one passage which might be classified as a formula citation in Mark; three in Luke; and, if the fulfillment sayings are counted, nine in John's gospel.[2] So the use of formula citations is a peculiarity of Matthew, and the presentation of the birth story as a fulfillment of the law and the prophets is Matthew's particular concern.

This important clue will help us examine in turn each episode in Matthew's Christmas story. There is no specific formula citation in the genealogy (1:1-17). However, the entire passage is a formalized scheme of Israelite history which traces, in a somewhat Procrustean manner, the descent of Jesus from Abraham, through David (see 1:17). It is, as Matthew states in verse 1, "the birth record of Jesus Christ, the son of David, the son of Abraham."

Matthew begins his birth story by answering the question, Who is Jesus? Through the genealogy he makes it clear that Jesus is both the son of David and, at the same time, the son of Abraham. He contends that Jesus is the son of David through the line of Joseph, his legal father. If you reread

Genesis 22:1-19 you will see what lies behind Matthew's claim that Jesus is also the son of Abraham. Genesis 22:18 contains the declaration that by Abraham and his offspring all the people of the world will bless themselves. So Matthew sees Jesus as the fulfillment of that promise. Jesus the descendant of Abraham offers messianic leadership to gentiles as well as Jews.

Comparing a passage in one gospel with a similar passage in another gospel is a useful way of discovering the uniqueness of each gospel's account. So in this case a comparison of Matthew's genealogy of Jesus with the genealogy in Luke 3:23-38 will be informative. Note, first, that Luke's genealogy is not part of his birth story at all. It is part of his account of Jesus' baptism. The scheme employed by Luke is the opposite of the approach taken by Matthew. Matthew traces the genealogy down from Abraham to David to Jesus. Luke starts with Jesus at the beginning of his public ministry and looks back to his ancestors. He traces Jesus' lineage all the way back to Adam, the mythic symbol of all humankind. Luke's point is that Jesus, the Son of God, is not some sort of a demigod but a person like all others, with a family tree. The fact that Jesus' ancestry stretches back to Adam emphasizes the universality of his ministry, an important theme—as we shall discover—in Luke's gospel. Note the difference, however, between this emphasis and the theme of the fulfillment of the law and the prophets which characterizes Matthew's gospel.

The second episode in Matthew's Christmas story, the account of the conception and birth of Jesus (1:18-25), is built around the formula citation in 1:22-23. Matthew again answers the question, Who is Jesus?, but this time at a more profound level. Jesus is not only the son of David, the son of Abraham. He is, more importantly, the Son of God. The tradition of the virginal conception suits Matthew's purpose here and becomes the vehicle by which he asserts that Jesus became the Son of God through the power of the Holy Spirit, not at his resurrection, nor even at his baptism, but from the very beginning at his birth.

We must take a careful look at Matthew 1:23 because

Matthew did not quote this passage from Isaiah 7:14 for the same reason that most people refer to it today. The modern emphasis is on the question, How did Jesus become the Son of God?, and attention is focused on the word "virgin" in this verse. In Hebrew the word is *almah,* and it means "a young woman of child bearing age." In the Greek version of the Old Testament this was translated *parthenos,* which means "virgin" in the usual sense. Christians, using the Greek version, have referred to this verse as a proof-text of the virginal conception.

But Matthew was not interested in that word at all. His question was not how, but who? Who is Jesus? He was concerned with the Hebrew word *Emmanuel.* He even goes to the trouble of translating it so that all his readers will be sure to understand it, "God-with-us." Emmanuel is Matthew's name for Jesus. It is his way of proclaiming the good news that Jesus is God-with-us, replacing the Jewish concept of the *shekinah,* the glorious presence of God in our midst hidden only by the splendor of light. If you look ahead in anticipation, you will discover that Matthew concludes his gospel the same way he begins it, with the promise that Jesus is with us always (28:20).

The reference to the name Jesus meaning "savior" in 1:21 is traditional. Matthew expects his readers, however, when they hear the name to remember Joshua, the successor of Moses. This is part of Matthew's technique. He not only uses formula citations to proclaim the meaning of Jesus' birth, but he also rings the changes on the law and the prophets in such a way that there are overtones which will be heard and understood by those who were brought up on the Jewish scriptures.

This is particularly true in the next episode in Matthew's Christmas story, his account of the visit of the Wise Men (2:1-12). Matthew uses the formula citation in 2:5-6 to answer the question, Where did all this happen? His answer is, of course, in Bethlehem in the days of Herod the king in fulfillment of the law and the prophets—specifically the prophecy of Micah 5:2 and 2 Samuel 5:2. A better translation of the final line in verse 6, one in keeping with 2 Samuel 5:2, is "who will *shepherd* my people Israel." So the Davidic Messiah comes not from Jerusalem but from Bethlehem. He is the king who comes to shepherd his people.

In addition to the fulfillment of the specific prophecy in the formula citation, there are echoes of many different Old Testament passages in the story of the visit of the Wise Men. For example, there are several references in the Old Testament to bringing gifts to the king. Psalm 72:10-11,15 speaks of gifts brought to the king at his enthronement. Isaiah 60:6 talks about bringing gold and frankincense from Sheba to Jerusalem. Psalm 45:8 describes the king being anointed with myrrh and other spices for his wedding. Matthew expected his readers to recall such passages from their Bible and understand that the Wise Men were paying homage to the newly enthroned Messiah.

The story is obviously legendary. Most likely it grew out of the tales of Balaam in Numbers 22-24. There is a direct reference in Numbers 24:17, in one of the blesssings that Balaam gives to Israel, to the rising in the future of a star and a scepter. This is the promise which seems to have fostered the story of the Wise Men who came, following a star. Matthew would be amused by the modern attempts to identify the astronomical phenomenon. For him it was the fulfillment of the law and the prophets, in this case Numbers 24:17.

The legend of the visit of the Wise Men is also important to Matthew because it is an example of non-Jews who came to pay homage to the Messiah. Jesus is not only the son of David, he is also the son of Abraham.

The fourth and final segment of Matthew's Christmas story, the episode of the flight to Egypt and the return to Nazareth (2:13-23), is based on three formula citations—2:15, 2:17-18, and 2:23. In this account Matthew answers the question, From where did Jesus come? The tradition said that, although Jesus was born in Bethlehem, he came from Nazareth. In this episode Matthew explains how, *and why,* Jesus goes from Bethlehem to Nazareth by way of Egypt.

There is no historical evidence to support the events in these scenes. Herod's actions are quite plausible, however. He was an Idumean and hence suspected by the Jews over whom he reigned. His position on the throne was precarious. He owed his power to the Romans, and he had to steer a dangerous course during the struggle for control of the empire between Antony and Octavian. At one time he almost lost much of his kingdom to Cleopatra, that woman from Egypt whom both Antony and Octavian found attractive.

Visitors to Israel today can see plenty of evidence of the fortified palaces Herod erected during his troubled rule. They dot the landscape. Almost every pilgrim goes to Masada, the most famous of Herod's fortresses. The Herodium, where tradition says Herod is buried, still stands as a silent sentinel, ironically keeping watch over Bethlehem and the surrounding territory.

Herod's anger is also quite in character. He tended to do away with anyone he thought was a threat to his throne, including some of the members of his own family. He drowned two of his sons by his first wife in the pool of his palace in Jericho. So he could have ordered the slaughter of the young boys in Bethlehem.

None of this is of interest to Matthew, however. He recounts this incident to give the reason for the flight of the Holy Family to Egypt. The important point for Matthew is the fulfillment of the prophecy, "Out of Egypt have I called my son" (2:15). This is a quotation from Hosea 11:1. It is Hosea's pleasing, poetic image of the Exodus, the picture of God leading Israel out of Egypt like a father leads his son and teaches him to walk. Matthew sees Jesus as a new Moses who leads a new Exodus out of Egypt. The connection between Joseph in this story and an earlier Patriarch named Joseph and the similarity between Moses' escape from the wrath of Pharaoh and Jesus' flight from the anger of Herod are overtones in Matthew's story which he expects his readers to hear.

The reference in 2:18 to Rachel weeping for her children from Jeremiah 31:15 reminded Matthew's readers of the other great event in Israel's history, the Exile. Originally Ramah was associated with the territory of Benjamin, north of Jerusalem where present-day Ramallah is located (see 1 Samuel 10:2). Later tradition placed it near Bethlehem where modern tourists are shown the tomb of Rachel (see Genesis 35:16-20). This double identification suits Matthew's purpose of connecting the event of Jesus' birth in Bethlehem with the Exile. He expects his readers to remember that Jeremiah says Rachel is weeping for her children Joseph and Benjamin, who represent the northern tribes, which were carried off into exile when the Assyrians took Samaria near the end of the eighth century B.C.

So in the final episode of his Christmas story Matthew proclaims Jesus as a new Moses who recapitulates for the new Israel the crucial experiences of the Exodus and the Exile.

The return to Nazareth, according to Matthew, also fulfills a prophecy. The connection, however, between Nazareth and the citation in 2:23, "He shall be called a Nazarene," is not clear. We do not know the source of this quotation. There are various possibilities. "Nazarene" might be related to the term "Nazarite" (see Judges 16:17) or to those called holy (see Isaiah 4:3). There is also the possibility that the word "Nazarene" could be related to the word *netzer,* which means "branch." If so, this quotation would be a reference to Isaiah 11:1, the prophecy of a branch that would grow out of the root of Jesse, the father of David. Even if the reference is obscure, the point Matthew makes is plain. Jesus returns to Nazareth and grows up there in fulfillment of the law and the prophets.

Geography is never simply geography in the gospels. So for Matthew, Galilee has a special significance. In Matthew 4:15 he calls it "Galilee of the Gentiles (see Isaiah 9:1)." For him, then, the return of Jesus to Nazereth underscores the fact that the Messiah, who was born according to the promise of the Jewish scriptures in the city of David, grew up in gentile Galilee.

What inferences can we draw then from our examination of Matthew's Christmas story? First, it appears that Matthew composed his gospel for a community made up largely of Jewish Christians with some gentile converts. His constant references to the Old Testament presuppose a congregation trained in the Jewish scriptures. Yet he is careful to translate the Hebrew word *Emmanuel* for his gentile readers. He proclaims Jesus as the son of David and the son of Abraham who was born in Bethlehem but grew up in Galilee of the gentiles.

Second, central to Matthew's purpose is his proclamation that Jesus is the fulfillment of the law and the prophets. Jesus is the new Moses. He recapitulates both the Exodus and the Exile. Most important for Matthew, Jesus is God-with-us, the fulfillment of the Jewish concept of the *shekinah*.

Third, Matthew's birth story is an integral part of his gospel. It introduces the basic theme and proclaims the central message of the gospel. It is a magnificent preparation for the story of the ministry of Jesus which begins with Matthew's account of his baptism in chapter 3 of the gospel.

What have we learned so far about a different method of studying the gospels by letting Matthew's Christmas story speak for itself?

We have discovered the importance of isolating the birth story in this gospel. On the one hand, this enabled us to observe more clearly the use Matthew made of traditional material. On the other hand, this underscored what was unique in Matthew's presentation of the infancy narrative. Most important, it helped us identify Matthew's stylistic peculiarity, the use of formula citations. This turned out to be a significant clue to the way Matthew told his Christmas story.

We have also learned, in our brief survey of the genealogies in Matthew and Luke, that comparing similar passages in different gospels can be a useful way of discovering the particular meaning of each gospel account.

We shall continue to apply these techniques of isolating and comparing material as we proceed. The unique character of Matthew's birth story will become even more apparent when we examine next the Christmas story of Luke.

Luke's Christmas Story

Considering the birth stories separately and then comparing them underscores the differences between them. But before we can compare the two versions of the infancy narrative, we must let Luke's Christmas story speak for itself.

A rereading of Luke 1 and 2 will remind you that Luke has organized the material in his story with the skill of a master craftsman. He begins with parallel accounts of two annunciations: first, the annunciation of the birth of John the Baptist (1:5-25) and, then, the annunciation of the birth of Jesus (1:26-38). This is followed by a description of the visitation of Elizabeth by Mary (1:39-56) which rounds out the first cycle of Luke's narrative.

This pattern is repeated in the second part of his story which begins with the account of the birth, circumcision, and naming of John the Baptist (1:57-80) followed by the parallel account of the birth, circumcision, and naming of Jesus (2:1-21). This cycle concludes with the story of the presentation of the infant Jesus in the temple (2:22-40).

Luke could have ended his birth narrative here. (Note the conclusion in 2:39-40 and compare these verses with 2:51-52, a second conclusion patterned on the previous one.) Presumably he added the episode of Jesus' visit to the temple when he was twelve (2:41-52) as an interlude between his birth story proper and his account of the ministry of Jesus which he begins in chapter 3.

A special feature of Luke's birth story is the addition of the beautiful canticles which he incorporates into his narrative (1:46-55, 1:67-79, 2:28-32, and 2:13-14). The first three are familiar to Christians because they have become part of the daily hours of prayer and praise. They are known by the initial word in the Latin version of each canticle: the *Magnificat,* the *Benedictus,* and the *Nunc Dimittis.* Originally these were hymns composed in the Semitic style by Jewish Christians. Luke uses them very effectively to punctuate his narrative.

The episode of Jesus' birth (2:1-20) is the climax of Luke's narrative, and to many Christians this single incident is the Christmas story. We must look closely at two references in this account which are generally misunderstood.

The first is the reference in 2:7 to Jesus being laid in a

manger. Modern readers focus their attention on the last phrase in the verse, "because there was no place for them in the inn." Many Christmas pageants dramatize the heartless innkeeper refusing entrance to Joseph and Mary. (Ironically, during a recent Christmas season when there was a drop in the tourist trade, the mayor of Bethlehem complained that there was too much room in the inn!)

Luke, on the other hand, places his emphasis on the preceding phrase, "and laid him in a manger." The important point is not that there was no room in the inn but that the infant had a manger for his bed. Jesus was laid in a manger because, as the Greek version of Isaiah 1:3 says, "The ox knows its owner/And the ass the manger of the Lord." The manger, since it was considered the "manger of the Lord," was regarded as a prophetic sign, and the placing of the child in the manger identified him as the Messiah (see 2:12). The swaddling cloths were also a sign. Even kings like Solomon were "nursed with care in swaddling cloths" (see Wisdom 7:4-5). Strangers and travelers stayed in the inn, the caravansary. Not Jesus. He was the promised Messiah, and so was wrapped in swaddling cloths and laid in the manger of the Lord.

The other reference is in 2:8-18, to the shepherds who came to visit the newborn child. Contemporary readers picture a pastoral scene and shepherds kneeling by the Christmas crib. Luke is probably alluding, however, to the "Tower of the Flock," in Hebrew the *Migdal Eder,* a title he assigns to Bethlehem. The allusion is to Micah 4:8, which identifies Jerusalem as the Tower of the Flock, plus Genesis 35:21, which transfers this title to Bethlehem. So just as Wise Men came to visit the child in Matthew's birth story in fulfillment of the prophecy in Numbers 24:17, so shepherds came to the manger in Luke's account because Bethlehem is the Tower of the Flock.

Now that we have familiarized ourselves with Luke's Christmas story we can compare it to Matthew's version. The contrast will reveal the unique characteristics of Luke's infancy narrative.

There are, of course, some basic similarities. Both

evangelists follow the tradition that Jesus was born in Bethlehem and grew up in Nazareth. But Luke does not handle the association of Jesus with these two places the same way Matthew does. As we have seen, according to Matthew, Joseph and Mary live in Bethlehem, and Jesus is born, presumably, in Joseph's house. The family moves to Nazareth when they return from Egypt after the death of Herod the Great.

Luke, on the other hand, places Mary and Joseph in Nazareth at the beginning of his birth story. They travel to Bethlehem, Joseph's ancestral home, to enroll in a census, and Jesus is born while they are there. At a suitable time the family returns to Nazareth, stopping in Jerusalem to present the child in the temple.

Both evangelists also use the tradition of the virginal conception to explain who Jesus is. Luke articulates this tradition in his account of the annunciation of the birth of Jesus (see 1:35). This verse recalls Isaiah 11:2 and Isaiah 4:2-3, passages which proclaim the prophetic promise of the coming of the branch of the Lord, the shoot from the stump of Jesse upon whom the Spirit of the Lord shall rest. Luke's purpose in telling the story of the annunciation is theological. We know from Romans 1:3-4 that in the earliest tradition Jesus was designated Son of God by the Spirit at his resurrection. Later tradition associated this identification of Jesus as the Son of God with his baptism (see Mark 1:9-11). Luke, like Matthew, pushes this designation back to the birth of Jesus.

There are, however, more differences than similarities between Matthew's infancy narrative and Luke's version of the story. In addition to the different way each evangelist identifies Jesus with Bethlehem and Nazareth, noted above, each gospel has a different focus for the story. Matthew makes Joseph the central character of his account. Luke emphasizes Mary. Herod the Great plays a major role in Matthew's story, but he is only mentioned once in Luke's version (see Luke 1:5). Luke makes John the Baptist a prominent actor in his narrative, but he never appears in Matthew's account.

The most notable feature of Luke's story is his addition

of a universal dimension to the narrative. The birth of Jesus, for him, is not an obscure event. It takes place at the center of the stage of world history. All the world is enrolled at the command of Caesar Augustus himself (2:1-2). The final scene in the drama takes place in the temple in Jerusalem where Jesus is proclaimed "a light for revelation to the Gentiles," that is, "the nations" (2:32). For Luke the birth of Jesus has universal implications.

For Luke, too, Jerusalem and the temple are significant symbols. Zechariah is serving as a priest in the temple when he is told about the birth of John the Baptist. Although Jesus is born in Bethlehem, he is brought to the temple in Jerusalem as soon as possible to be presented to the Lord (2:22-40). Luke also adds the episode of the visit of Jesus to the temple at the age of twelve (2:41-52) which reenforces the association of Jesus with Jerusalem. By contrast, in Matthew, Jerusalem is the seat of Herod, and Joseph avoids the city in order to protect Mary and Jesus.

Luke does not use the formula citations so characteristic of Matthew. There are, of course, many allusions to the Old Testament in Luke's infancy narrative. Zechariah and Elizabeth represent the faithful remnant of Israel, and the story of the birth of their son is reminiscent of the stories of the wonderful births of Samuel and Isaac. John the Baptist is identified, in keeping with the tradition, as an Elijah. Luke 1:32-33 in the account of the annunciation of the birth of Jesus reminds us of the promise in 2 Samuel 7:8-16 which identifies the child to be born as the long awaited Davidic Messiah. Luke's expression of the tradition of the virginal conception (1:35) recalls Isaiah 11:1-2 and Isaiah 4:2-3. In recounting the episode of Jesus' birth (2:1-20) Luke makes use of the symbols of the manger, based on Isaiah 1:3, and the Tower of the Flock, based on Micah 4:8 and Genesis 35:21, as we noted above. In 2:11 there are echoes of Isaiah 9:6, and overtones of Isaiah 52:7 and Isaiah 61:1 in 2:10. Luke used a source here which was strongly influenced by the prophetic promises of the Old Testament.

You will notice, however, that Luke never claims that all this happens in fulfillment of the law and the prophets as Matthew does. In the episode of the presentation of Jesus in the temple (2:22-40) — which may have been modeled on the story of the presentation of Samuel in the sanctuary in Shiloh (see 1 Samuel 1:21-28) — the important point for Luke is not the fulfillment of the law but the manifestation of the child who is a light for revelation to the nations as well as for glory to the people of Israel (2:32).

Matthew's infancy narrative is an integral part of his gospel, but the birth story was not originally part of Luke's gospel. Notice that Luke portrays John the Baptist differently in Chapters 1 and 2 from the way he describes him in the rest of the gospel. In the birth narrative, John the Baptist is identified as a relative of Jesus. Elizabeth, his mother, is described as Mary's kinswoman (1:36). It is prophesied that John the Baptist will go before Jesus "in the spirit and power of Elijah" (1:17). Compare this picture of the Baptist with that in Luke 7:18-23 where John seems uncertain of the identity of Jesus. Note also that in Luke 16:16 John the Baptist is described as the last prophet in the epoch before the birth of Jesus, not as his forerunner!

Luke 3 is obviously a new beginning, and verses 1 and 2 make an impressive introduction to the gospel. In addition, certain characteristics of Luke 1-2 are more like the material in Acts than the rest of Luke's gospel. These include references to the outpouring of the Spirit, the angelic appearances, and the use of the title, "Christ the Lord."[3] It appears that Luke added the birth story as a prologue to his gospel when he wrote Acts, the second volume of his work.

We can draw several inferences from our examination of Luke's Christmas story. Luke is writing for gentile Christians in the wide world of his day. Jerusalem and especially the temple have a symbolic meaning for his readers. So Luke's birth story forms an admirable preface not just to his story of the ministry of Jesus but, more particularly, to his description in Acts of the spread of the gospel from Jerusalem to Rome.

Finally, we can see that Luke, like Matthew, has a theological purpose in telling his story of Jesus' birth. He, too, employs the tradition of the virginal conception of Jesus to make it clear that Jesus was the Son of God from his birth. But Luke, unlike Matthew, sees the birth of Jesus as the inauguration of a new and decisive epoch in the story of the world. For him Jesus is at the center of history.

We have arrived at this understanding of Luke's Christmas story by the simple method of comparing it to Matthew's infancy narrative. The contrast has revealed the unique characteristics of Luke's birth story.

If you were surprised by the difference between the Christmas stories of Matthew and Luke, prepare yourself for a more amazing discovery. The Christmas stories of Mark and John, which we shall consider next, are not birth stories at all.

John's Christmas Story

The Christmas stories of John and Mark were determined by the liturgical use of the church. In the West, the gospel reading appointed by the church for the principal service on the feast of the Nativity is the prologue to John's gospel (1:1-18).

This passage is so different from the Christmas stories of Matthew and Luke that there is no difficulty letting it speak for itself. It is obviously not a birth story. There is no mention of Bethlehem or Nazareth. There is no reference to Herod the Great or Augustus Caesar. There is no story about shepherds or Wise Men. In fact there is no mention of Jesus by name. The only historical figure identified in this account is John the Baptist, and the references to him are in parenthetical sections of the prologue (see 1:6-8 and 1:15). If we possessed only John's gospel, we would have no historical information about the birth of Jesus.

Why, we may ask, did the church in the West choose this reading for the gospel lesson on Christmas Day? To answer this question let us examine John 1:1-18 more closely. We will have to identify the form and structure of this passsage in order to understand its meaning and purpose. Then we shall be able to comprehend why its message is considered *the* Christmas story by a great segment of the church.

The prologue to John's gospel is a hymn. It was sung by early Christians to proclaim Jesus' special relationship to God, and it was part of the traditional material John used to compose his gospel. It is similar to two hymns in the Pauline literature, one which celebrates Jesus as the Christ "who though he was in the form of God...emptied himself taking the form of a servant" (read Philippians 2:6-11), and the other which praises Jesus as "the image of the invisible God, the firstborn of all creation" (read Colossians 1:15-20). John used this hymn to the incarnate Word to introduce his gospel.

The structure of the passage is quite simple. The hymn celebrates the Word in four stanzas—1:1-2, which speaks of the pre-existent Word with God; 1:3-5, which associates the Word with creation; 1:10-12, which speaks of the Word in the world; and 1:14,16, which proclaims the incarnation of the Word.

The hymn is interrupted by references to John the Baptist (1:6-9 and 1:15), and it is augmented by some explanatory material (1:12c—"who believed in his name"—and 13, plus 1:17-18).

The key to the meaning and purpose of the passage lies in the central term "Word." This is the English translation of the Greek *logos* which stands for an important concept in Stoic and Neo-Platonic thought. So interpreters originally searched these philosophies for the meaning of this term. Recent scholarship has demonstrated, however, that the background of this hymn is predominantly Semitic. So we shall turn to the Jewish thought of the period to try to understand the meaning of this term.

In biblical Hebrew usage the term "word," *davar,* means not only something spoken but also something done. The association between word and event is very close. In the first account of creation in Genesis (see 1:1-2:3) God simply speaks and it is accomplished: "And God said, Let there be light,

And there was light" (1:3). In this connection, notice the deliberate parallelism between the opening verse of John's prologue and the first verse of Genesis.

In Semitic speech a word has a reality of its own. A blessing given by mistake to Jacob by Isaac cannot simply be repeated when Esau shows up. That word is gone, and Esau must content himself with a different blessing (see Genesis 27:1-40). The word of God, then, is objective and creative. It goes forth from God's mouth to accomplish his purpose (see Isaiah 55:11).

The term "word" has three important associations in the Old Testament, and these associations correspond to the three sections of the Hebrew Bible—the Torah, the Prophets, and the Writings. The Torah can be distilled into the Ten Commandents, more properly called the Decalogue, the "Ten Words." The prophets are God's spokesmen who proclaim his words. The word is the word of wisdom.

This last association of word with wisdom is particularly important for our understanding of John's prologue. In the Wisdom literature there is a gradual personification of wisdom, until Wisdom, now spelled with a capital W, is almost equivalent to God. Proverbs 1:20-33 portrays Wisdom as a street vendor hawking her wares in the city gate. The Book of Wisdom 7:22b-8:1 is an exquisite paean to Wisdom, praising her in the same exalted way the Word is celebrated in John 1:1-18.[4]

The point of the hymn is that this pre-existent Word "became flesh and dwelt among us" (John 1:14). The term "flesh" is a graphic expression meaning "human" (see Romans 1:3 and 8:3 for examples of this usage in the tradition as early as Paul). The term "dwelt" literally means "tented" or "tabernacled," and it is related to the Hebrew word *shekinah* and the concept it expressed. John used this hymn, then, to contradict the gnostic, docetic notion that Jesus was not truly human, while at the same time proclaiming his unique relationship to God from the very beginning, from before creation itself. John found the tradition of the incarnate, pre-existent Word made to order for his high christology, that is, his theological understanding of Jesus which emphasized Jesus' divine nature.

The Fourth Evangelist also used this hymn to introduce some of his basic themes. The theme of light versus darkness (see 1:4-5 and 1:7-9) plays a major part in John's gospel. The struggle between the forces of light and the forces of darkness was the central focus of the apocalyptic thought which permeated the first century A.D. The Dead Sea Scrolls have documented the significance this kind of thinking had for the Judaism from which Christianity emerged.

Two terms which are important in John's theological vocabulary are introduced in the prologue. The first of these is "grace" which is the Greek equivalent of the Hebrew *chesed,* a reference to God's responsible love. The other is "truth," in Hebrew *emeth,* which is used in an existential sense to emphasize the relationship of trust between God and us, a relationship based on God's faithfulness (see 1:14-16). Both are embodied by Jesus, the incarnate Word.

Although his purpose was the same as Matthew's and Luke's, namely, to proclaim that Jesus is the Son of God from the very beginning, John found a way to do this which was more emphatic. He composed his gospel for a community engaged in theological reflection about Jesus at a more advanced stage. His choice of the hymn to the incarnate Word proved to have appeal to the wider Hellenistic thought world, probably because it was possible to identify the Word with the *logos* principle of Stoic and Neo-Platonic philosophy.

Later the church fused the theological reflection of Matthew and Luke, based on the tradition of the virginal conception of Jesus, with the theological reflection of John, based on the tradition of the incarnate, pre-existent Word, into a single statement. The Nicene Creed says Jesus became incarnate "from the Virgin Mary" and was made man. We are most familiar with this final form of the theological reflection on the birth of Jesus.

It is easy to see why John 1:1-8 became the gospel reading

on Christmas Day for the church in the West. The church focused its celebration on the birth of Jesus, but it opted for a theological emphasis over an historical one. John's prologue was clearly the best way to say this.

If you are used to the Western rite, you were not too surprised to learn that John 1:1-18 is a Christmas story. It is not immediately apparent, however, how any passage in Mark could be so designated. Even the suggestion that Mark tells a Christmas story demands some explanation, and to that task we turn next.

Mark's Christmas Story

How can Mark tell a Christmas story when he begins his gospel with the account of Jesus' public ministry? The answer to our question comes, again, from the liturgical use of the church. In the East, the church focuses on the celebration of the Epiphany, not the Nativity, and the traditional gospel reading for that liturgy is the story of the baptism of Jesus. This is *the* story of the manifestation of Jesus, the Christ, to the world.

Mark makes this event the center of the opening story of his gospel (see 1:1-15, particularly 1:9-11). This inaugural story performs the same function as the birth stories in Matthew and Luke and the hymn to the incarnate Word in John. It declares the good news that Jesus is designated the Son of God by the Spirit from the beginning. For Mark this beginning is the start of Jesus' ministry. So in this sense Mark 1:1-15 is a Christmas story, particularly associated with the celebration of this feast by the church in the East.

Mark 1:1-15 can best be understood by examining the passage backwards. 1:14-15 announces the inauguration of Jesus' public ministry, a ministry which proclaims that the kingdom of God is at hand and calls all to repentance and belief in this good news. The reader is prepared for this announcement by the reference to the temptation of Jesus in the widerness in 1:12-13. This incident, in turn, is the result of the baptism of Jesus described in 1:9-11. Here Mark employs a tradition which identifies Jesus as the Messiah who suffers. 1:11 contains a quotation from Psalm 2:7 which is the enthronement formula for the king, the Messiah, and a reference to Isaiah 42:1, the opening verse of a song about the suffering servant. The preaching of John the Baptist (1:7-8) is understood as a preparation for the baptism Jesus will bring, and John's ministry is introduced by a description of his appearance in the wilderness (1:4-6). Mark identifies the theological implications of the reference to the wilderness by the quotations from Malachi 3:1 and Isaiah 40:3 in 1:2-3. The purpose of the whole passage is proclaimed in 1:1. The opening verse is, as it were, Mark's last word in the passage. This, then, is Mark's inaugural story by which he introduces Jesus as the Messiah, the Son of God.

Mark differs from Matthew and Luke, who use his gospel as one of their main sources, in the meaning he gives to the term "gospel" and the role he assigns to John the Baptist.

Mark introduces the term "gospel" from the missionary vocabulary of the Pauline letters. For Mark, as for Paul, Jesus himself is the gospel. "Jesus" and "gospel" are synonymous. See the phrase "for my sake and the gospel's" in Mark 8:35 and 10:29, for example. The words "and the gospel's" are missing from the parallel passages of these sayings in Matthew and Luke.

For Mark, the gospel *re-presents* the risen Lord to those who hear it. This is the significance of the gospel reading in the liturgy today and the reason for the gospel procession and the rites venerating the gospel book. The gospel is a sign of the presence of the risen Christ in the liturgy. In contrast, in Matthew's gospel Jesus proclaims the gospel. Luke avoids the term "gospel." For him Jesus is the center of history.

We shall reserve comment on the message the risen Christ proclaims in Mark's gospel until we have examined his story of the resurrection and the crucifixion. Then we shall be able to understand why the proclamation in 1:15 that the time is fulfilled and the kingdom is at hand has a special meaning for Mark. He sees it as the announcement of the Second Coming of the risen Lord rather than the beginning of Jesus' public ministry. For Mark, Jesus is an eschatological prophet.

Mark describes John the Baptist as a collaborator of Jesus. Both John and Jesus are in the wilderness. Both proclaim the kingdom and preach repentance. Both are "delivered up" to death. By contrast, in Matthew's gospel John the Baptist is an Elijah figure, a forerunner of Jesus. In John's gospel this role is more fully developed. John recognizes Jesus as the Lamb of God at the very beginning of this gospel. Yet John was not the light but the witness to the light. In Luke's gospel proper John the Baptist belongs to the period of Israel which precedes the period of Jesus' ministry. John is the last great figure in the epoch that is past.

From our examination of Mark's Christmas story we can infer, first, that Mark has the same theological purpose, in general, as the other evangelists in telling his inaugural story. He wants to make it clear that Jesus is the Son of God from the beginning. In contradiction to the notion of adoptionism, Jesus did not become the Son of God at his resurrection. Second, for Mark, Jesus is the Messiah who suffers and dies. We shall keep these inferences in mind as we examine Mark's Easter and Good Friday stories in the following chapters.

We began our comparison of the gospels with a careful look at the Christmas story in each.[5] This was a convenient place to start because it provided you with an introduction to the method of study which lets each gospel speak for itself.

Now we shall have to turn to the end of the gospels and compare the accounts of the crucifixion and the resurrection. For the evangelists this was the beginning of the story of Jesus. The gospels were composed from the perspective of those who knew and believed in the risen Lord. For the evangelists, as indeed for all Christians, the resurrection was the foundation for their faith. So we shall examine next the Easter story in each of the four gospels.

2

The Easter Stories

Each gospel tells the Easter story in its own way, but one episode, the account of the empty tomb, occurs in all four gospels. The tradition of the empty tomb is not part of the earliest Easter story, which records only appearances of the risen Christ (see 1 Corinthians 15:3-8). It is undoubtedly a tradition of the church in Jerusalem where the location of the tomb was known, remembered, and later venerated. The episode of the empty tomb is the entire Easter story in Mark (16:1-8) since Mark's gospel ends abruptly with 16:8 (verses 9-20 are a late appendix).

A COMPARISON OF THE EMPTY TOMB ACCOUNTS IN THE FOUR GOSPELS

MARK 16:1-8	MATTHEW 28:1-10	LUKE 24:1-11	JOHN 20:1-10
v.1 Women who witnessed the burial—Mary Magdalene, Mary the mother of James, Salome—bring spices to anoint his body.	Mary Magdalene, the other Mary	women from Galilee—Mary Magdalene, Joanna, Mary the mother of James, other women (v.10) with spices	Mary Magdalene (burial completed Friday Jn. 19: 38-42)
v.2 very early, first day of the week	toward dawn, first day of the week	early dawn, first day of the week	early, while still dark, first day of the week
v.3-4 Who will *roll* away the stone? found it done	earthquake, angel *rolled* away stone	found stone *rolled* away (no mention of sealing tomb with stone)	saw stone *taken* away (no mention of sealing tomb with stone)
v.5 young man in white	angel, raiment white as snow	two men in dazzling apparel	John very different—Mary Magdalene gets Peter and Beloved Disciple who come to the tomb and enter (Peter first). Peter saw, Beloved Disciple saw and believed.

v.5 women amazed	guards afraid, women afraid, of angel	women perplexed, frightened by two men
v.6 "He has risen, he is not here."	"He is not here, he has risen."	"Why do you seek the living among the dead?" (24:5)
v.7 Tell his disciples and Peter that *he is going before you to Galilee*.	Tell his disciples *that he has risen from the dead*, and ...he is going before you to Galilee.	reference in 24:6 to a saying of Jesus when he was in Galilee (Son of man saying) 24:7
v.8 Women fled in fear and trembling, said nothing to anyone	Women went with fear and *great joy*, ran to tell disciples; met risen Christ who repeats message.	women told eleven and all the rest. Apostles dismissed their words as an idle tale (24:9-11)
		(Cf. 20:9 – as yet they did not know the scripture that he must rise from the dead.)
		No mention of Galilee, disciples went back to their homes in Jerusalem

Mark's Easter Story

Because the account of the empty tomb is common to the four gospels, it provides us with an exercise in the critical method we are using. We can compare the four versions of this narrative to discover what is unique in the account of each of the gospels. This is an awkward process unless you have a parallel version of the gospels. So, to assist you in this a chart has been prepared. To use it, open your Bible to Mark 16:1-8 and follow Mark's version of the story noted in the left-hand column of the chart. By looking across the chart at each of the other columns you will be able to see the differences in the versions of Matthew, Luke, and John. As you work through this comparison keep asking yourself, What is unique or different in Mark's account of the empty tomb?

If you allow for minor variations and take into consideration the very different form of the account of this episode in John's gospel, three unique features of Mark's version emerge. The first of these is the emphasis on the amazement, fear, and trembling of the women (see 16:5-6 and 8). Their astonishment left them speechless, and they did not carry out the order to deliver the message to Peter and the other disciples.

The abrupt conclusion of Mark's gospel with the statement that the women were afraid (16:8) fits the context in which Mark sets his passion narrative and Easter story (14-16). Mark 13, the "Marcan Apocalypse," gives an eschatological introduction to these chapters. This chapter is Mark's composition, based on the Jewish apocalyptic tradition, which foresees the destruction of the Jerusalem temple (see 13:2-3) and reflects the circumstances of the Jewish War from A.D. 66 to 70 (see 13:5-13). This is Mark's description of the beginning of the End, that is, the *eschaton,* the end of the world. It is a sermon on the imminent expectation of the Second Coming of Christ, the *Parousia,* delivered by the risen Lord himself.[1]

The second distinctive feature of Mark's account of the empty tomb is the particular reference to Galilee in 16:7. Notice how this verse interrupts verses 6 and 8 and contradicts verse 8. The phrase "as he told you" in verse 7 refers to the promise

Jesus makes to his disciples, in Mark's version of the passion narrative, that he will go before them into Galilee (see Mark 14:28). Matthew who follows his Marcan source closely in the passion narrative, echoes this reference (see Matthew 26:32 and 28:7). But Luke handles it very differently, making the reference to Galilee a reminder of a saying of Jesus during his ministry in Galilee (see Luke 24:6).

Why is Galilee so important to Mark? Of course there is an historical basis for this interest. A great part of Jesus' ministry was in Galilee. Mark, however, organized his sources so that Jesus remains in Galilee for his entire ministry. In Mark's gospel Jesus goes to Jerusalem only once, for his crucifixion, and then by way of Perea, part of the tetrarchy of Galilee. Then immediately after his resurrection the disciples are commanded to return to Galilee. Chapters 1-9 in Mark are set in Galilee. Chapter 10 is a transition to chapters 11-16, which describe the events during the last week of Jesus' ministry when he was in Jerusalem. Mark deliberately composed a "Galilean Gospel."

The other evangelists do not place so much emphasis on Galilee. Although Matthew and Luke follow, in general, the scheme laid out by Mark, they make some interesting modifications. According to Matthew, Jesus ministers in Galilee to fulfill the law and the prophets and to show that his mission was to gentiles as well as Jews. Luke, who is not too precise about geography, is more concerned with the people than the place. Luke portrays the Galileans as the witnesses who go up to Jerusalem with Jesus. Jerusalem is the central focus of the gospel.

John does not follow Mark's scheme of organization at all. According to the Fourth Gospel, Jesus makes several journeys to Jerusalem during his ministry.[2]

So Galilee means something special to Mark. Is it significant because, possibly, the Jerusalem community of Christians was dispersed there during the troubled times between A.D. 66 and 70? Or, is "Galilee" a symbol of the dispersed church facing a period of turmoil—such as the church in Rome during the Neronian persecution in the 60s—a troubled time that looks like the End?

The third unique feature of Mark's account of the empty tomb is the absence of any reference to the resurrection in the message the women were commanded to deliver to the apostles (16:7). The omission is more glaring when we compare the parallel verse in Matthew's gospel where the women are directed to tell the disciples, first of all, that Jesus has risen from the dead (Matthew 28:7).

All these pieces of evidence—the fear of the women, the particular reference to Galilee, and the omission of any mention of the resurrection in the message entrusted to the women—fit together neatly if we take seriously the apocalyptic context Mark supplies in Chapter 13 for his story of the crucifixion and the resurrection.

Mark's Easter story, then, is a proclamation, not of the resurrection, but of the *Parousia,* the Second Coming of Christ. There is no need for recounting the tradition of the appearances of the risen Christ. He himself will come, soon, to his dispersed church in Galilee, which could be a reference either to Galilee proper or to a persecuted congregation such as that in Rome which is facing what looks like the End. The abruptness of the ending of Mark's gospel only increases the anticipation with which his readers look forward to the coming, momentarily, of their risen Lord.

It is in this context that we can understand how, for Mark, the proclamation in Mark 1:15 refers, not to Jesus' public ministry, but to his Second Coming. This interpretation will be supported by our examination of Mark's passion narrative in the following chapter.

This little exercise in the critical method we are using demonstrates how important it is to let each gospel speak for itself. At the same time it illustrates how this can be done, that is, by isolating and comparing the four gospel versions of an episode.

So we must continue our comparison of the Easter stories in the other gospels. We shall turn next to Matthew's Easter story. Because Matthew uses Mark as one of his main sources, the way Matthew modifies and amplifies this source will underscore both the unique apocalyptic emphasis of Mark's Easter story and the distinctive features of Matthew's story of the resurrection.

Matthew's Easter Story

All four evangelists tell the story of the empty tomb. For Mark this is the entire Easter story, but for the other three gospel writers it is only the first episode. It serves as an introduction to their accounts of the appearances of the risen Christ. In our examination of Matthew's Easter story, therefore, we shall look briefly at his additions to Mark's account of the empty tomb (28:1-15). Then we shall concentrate on the account of the appearance of the risen Christ to the Eleven in Galilee, an incident unique to Matthew's gospel (28:16-20). This will allow Matthew to tell the story of the resurrection in his own way.

Matthew uses Mark's account of the empty tomb as his primary source for this incident. A review of the chart earlier in this chapter will refresh your memory about the additions Matthew makes to Mark's story. Some are only minor modifications. In 28:2-3 Matthew replaces Mark's young man in white with an angel of the Lord and adds details about an earthquake which explain how the stone was rolled away from the tomb. Such elaborations of Mark's account seem characteristic of Matthew's story of the crucifixion and the resurrection (compare Matthew 27:51-54 with Mark 15:38, for example).

Some additions, though minor, create a major shift in emphasis in the account of this episode. In 28:7 Matthew adds the important phrase, "that he has risen from the dead" to the message entrusted to the women. As we noted above, this completely changes the emphasis Mark placed on the message. It is no longer a command to return to Galilee to wait for the coming of the risen Christ. Now it is a proclamation of the good news that Jesus has risen from the dead. In Matthew 28:8 the women depart with fear *and great joy* and *run* to tell the disciples the good news. This simple addition radically alters the mood of the scene, changing it from fear to excitement and joy. Matthew also reenforced the command to the women by describing the appearance to them of the risen Christ (28:9-10) who repeats the directive to inform the disciples, telling them explicitly not to be afraid.

So in Matthew's version of this incident Galilee is no longer so crucial. What matters is the good news that Jesus has risen. The women deliver this message which is cause for great rejoicing.

Matthew adds another incident to the story which describes the placing of Jewish guards at the tomb and their subsequent behavior (see 27:62-66 and 28:4,11-15). It was obviously a Christian apologetic designed to counteract the rumor, circulating in Matthew's day, that the disciples stole the body of Jesus and then claimed he had risen from the dead (see 28:11-15). Matthew was the only one of the four evangelists who was concerned with this rumor, and ultimately it seemed to have had little importance for the church.[3]

Matthew's distinctive addition to Mark's Easter story is his account of the enthronement of Jesus and the commissioning of the Eleven (28:16-20). The reference to "the eleven disciples" in 28:16 is an indication that we are dealing with material which uses established church terminology. By Matthew's time the Eleven, raised later to the proper number of twelve when Matthias replaced Judas (see Acts 1:15-26), was the technical term used to indicate the apostolic leaders of the church.

The reference to "the mountain" in 28:16 is very significant. The mountain in Galilee is not identified by name. It is simply called "*the* mountain." In Matthew's gospel the teachings of Jesus are presented in a sermon on the mount. As Moses received the Torah on the mountain, so Jesus, the new Moses, delivers the new Torah on the mount. Appropriately, then, Jesus is enthroned and his apostolic leaders are commissioned on the mountain. The mountain need not be identified geographically because for Matthew it has a symbolic meaning.

Matthew 28:18 is clearly the fulfillment of Daniel 7:14, the enthronement of the Messiah, and it is surprising that Matthew does not specify this. The traditional Jewish apocalyptic imagery adds a note of grandeur to this description of the appearance of the risen Christ to this disciples. Although some doubted (see 28:17),[4] Jesus' words convinced them, and they were commissioned to convert the world (28:19-20). Even though the liturgical formula in 28:19 reflects developed church usage, Matthew was thinking in rabbinic terms of the process of making disciples by proselyte baptism. The apostles were then directed to teach the proselytes to observe all that Jesus had commanded them, that is, the *mitzvot,* the commandments of the new Torah (28:20a).

Matthew concludes his gospel with the risen Christ's promise that he will be with his apostles "to the close of the age" (28:20b). Notice that in Matthew's gospel there is no eager anticipation of the imminent Second Coming of Jesus as there is in Mark. Nor is there any farewell from Jesus to his disciples as we shall discover in Luke and, to some degree, in John. Matthew emphasizes the promise of the risen Christ that he will be present in his church until the End.

This emphasis is quite in keeping with Matthew's claim that Jesus replaces the Jewish *shekinah,* the symbol of the presence of God in our midst. His particular name for Jesus at his birth was Emmanuel, God-with-us (see 1:23). Matthew makes the same point by portraying Jesus as the giver of the new Torah. In the Mishnah, part of the Jewish Talmud, the following Rabbinic saying *(Pirke Aboth* 3:2) is recorded: "If two sit together and there are words of Torah between them, the *shekinah* rests between them."

Turn to Matthew 18:19-20 and see how similar this rabbinic saying is to a familiar saying of Jesus: "If two of you agree on earth about anything they ask, it will be done for them by my Father in heaven, for where two or three are gathered in my name, there am I in the midst of them." You will not be surprised to learn that only Matthew records this saying of Jesus.

For Matthew, then, the risen Messiah is the new Moses who proclaims the new Torah with the new commandments from the sacred mountain. He is the new *shekinah,* the new presence of God in his church.

Matthew is not concerned very much with the Second Coming of Christ. Instead he emphasizes the mission of the church to the whole world and the promise of the presence of the risen Christ in the church until the new age comes. Matthew composed his gospel for a mixed Jewish-gentile Christian community to encourage this congregtion to carry out the mission of converting those like them dispersed in the Roman Empire.

So even though Matthew used Mark as his main source, he told a very different Easter story. We were able to discover this by isolating each account and comparing them. In this way we let each gospel speak for itself.

The other two evangelists, Luke and John, to whom we now turn, tell the Easter story in even more different ways. By isolating Luke's story of the resurrection next, we shall discover how unique it is.

Luke's Easter Story

Luke does not follow his Marcan source as closely as Matthew does. So he tells his own distinct version of the Easter story (24:1-53). The general structure of this chapter is the same as that of Matthew 28. It begins with the account of the discovery of the empty tomb (24:1-11), which serves as an introduction to the description of several appearances of the risen Christ (24:13-53). But there the similarity ends.

The episode of the empty tomb is not important to Luke. The two variations in his version of this account (see the chart earlier in this chapter) are evidence of this. First, the proclamation to the women at the tomb is different. It is in the form of a question, "Why do you seek the living among the dead?"

(24:5). There is no mention of the traditional news that Jesus is not there but has risen from the dead. The omission is so striking that some ancient textual authorities added these familiar words to Luke's account (see the last phrase of 24:5 in an English version without critical notes). Second, the apostles dismiss the report of the women who discovered the empty tomb as "an idle tale" (24:11).

Clearly, the tradition of the empty tomb has less significance for Luke than the tradition of the appearances of the risen Christ "among the living." So the important part of Luke's Easter story is his account of the appearances of Jesus after his resurrection.

There are three of these: the appearance to the men returning to Emmaus, which includes a reference to the appearance to Peter (24:13-35); the appearance to the Eleven, which includes the commissioning of the disciples (24:36-49); and the final appearance of the risen Christ at his ascension (24:50-53). Although they contain references to the traditional appearances to Peter and the apostolic leaders, all three episodes are unique to Luke's gospel. So an examination of them will show us the distinctive features of Luke's Easter story.

The accounts of the first two episodes have a similar structure and we can consider them together. To begin with, both episodes stress the tradition that the resurrection of Jesus fulfills the scriptures. Luke adds, as his distinctive emphasis, the point that only the risen Christ himself can interpret the scriptures correctly, that is, that the scriptures (the Old Testament) can only be understood in light of the resurrection (see 24:27 and 24:44-46).

In both accounts emphasis is placed on eating with the risen Christ (24:30 and 24:42-43). In fact in Luke's gospel this seems to be the central focus of the stories of the resurrection appearances of Jesus. The risen Lord is known "in the breaking of the bread" (24:35).

The account of eating fish with the disciples may have been introduced into the Easter tradition to counteract the docetic notion that the risen Christ did not appear in bodily form. So Jesus is described as a man with a body that can be handled and touched (24:39; see also John 20:20, 24-28 for similar references to touching). He was a hungry man who ate broiled fish for supper (24:41-43; see also John 21:9-14).

The Emmaus episode, however, places the emphasis on eating with the risen Lord in a liturgical context. Eucharistic language is used to describe the meal (notice 24:30 and 35). Moreover, the structure of this account follows the form of the eucharistic liturgy. First, the emphasis is on the word, the exposition of the scriptures, and then the episode reaches a climax in the breaking of the bread, the eucharist. This liturgical emphasis is in keeping with the way Luke introduces the parable of the great feast in his gospel (14:15-24): "Blessed is he who shall eat bread in the Kingdom of God" (Luke 14:15). Compare this with the different way Matthew introduces this same parable in his gospel (see Matthew 22:1-10). The word becomes intelligible only after the eyes of Cleopas and his companion have been opened to recognize Christ in the eucharistic action.

So, for Luke the eucharist is not a memorial of the last supper, an event that took place before Jesus' crucifixion. It is a feast in anticipation of the fulfillment of the kingdom. It is a joyous celebration of the future hope of the Christian community, and most importantly for Luke, it is a celebration in the presence of the risen Lord.

The third appearance story in Luke's gospel is one of his two versions of the ascension (24:50-53). The other account in Acts 1:1-11 is more likely to be the original version. The ascension story in the gospel is suspect on two counts. First, the reference to Bethany is unlikely. The tradition, favored in Acts, locates the episode on the Mount of Olives. Second, according to Luke the ascension is a prelude to the Pentecost experience rather than an Easter appearance of Christ.

Luke uses the episode of the ascension to separate the epoch of the ministry of Jesus from the epoch of the mission of the church. It is Jesus' farewell appearance. The only other reference to the ascension in the gospels is in the Fourth Gospel, but John, as we shall see when we examine this material, has a very different notion of the ascension.

So Luke is responsible for dividing the Easter story into three separate events: the resurrection, the ascension, and Pentecost. This scheme now dominates the church's worship, and it is the one with which modern Christians are most familiar. We take it so much for granted that we overlook the fact that the separation of the Easter event into three separate episodes is due to Luke's unique version of the story of the resurrection. No other gospel writer tells the Easter story this way.

We have isolated Luke's story of the resurrection and discovered that it has its own distinct features. It is clear that Luke is writing his gospel for Christians who are not much concerned about the empty tomb. Jerusalem is a symbol for them. His readers are also not anticipating the imminent end of the world. They are concerned with the future of history and their mission in the world.

By separating Easter from Pentecost with the account of the ascension, Luke emphasized the shift from the apocalyptic focus of Mark's gospel to the historical perspective which is characteristic of his gospel. Luke sees history spread out over time three periods: the epoch of Israel which culminates in the ministry of John the Baptist, the epoch of the ministry of Jesus from his birth to his resurrection, and the epoch of the mission of the church from Pentecost to the present. The ascension is his dividing line between the last two epochs.

On the one hand, Luke is anxious to explain to the church of his day why the risen Christ no longer appears as he once did after his resurrection. On the other hand, Luke wants to reassure his readers that the risen Lord is present with them in a different way. So he emphasizes the experience of eating with the risen Christ in his account of the resurrection appearances. Christians in all times and in all places will know the risen Lord in the breaking of the bread. Luke's version of the Easter story has left its mark on the church's calendar and on the eucharistic theology of the Christian community.

It is evident then that Luke told the story of the resurrection to encourage the church in its mission to the world (Luke 24:47) and in particular to remind his readers that, like the original apostles, they were "witnesses of these things" (24:48). Because we modern Christians see ourselves in much the same way as the congregation for which Luke composed his gospel, his Easter story seems to speak directly to us.

We shall turn, finally, to John's story of the resurrection and examine the distinctive features of this version of the Easter story by letting the Fourth Gospel speak for itself.

John's Easter Story

Since John's gospel is so different from the Synoptics, it is surprising that his Easter story is at all similar to theirs. All the gospel writers, however, follow the same basic tradition of the resurrection. Like Luke and Matthew, the Fourth Evangelist describes the Easter event in two stages, the discovery of the empty tomb (20:1-18) and the appearance of the risen Christ to his disciples (20:19-29). Although he builds his story of the resurrection on the traditional structure, John tells it in his own distinctive fashion. We shall examine, therefore, the material that is unique to the Fourth Gospel.

John's account of the discovery of the empty tomb is quite different from the episode in the Synoptic gospels (see the chart earlier in this chapter). To begin with, John's storytelling style is different. Throughout his gospel he achieves a vivid effect by focusing on just a few characters in each episode. This allows him to develop each character more fully and to create dramatic dialogue. In this episode he confines the cast of characters to Mary Magdalene, Peter, and "the other disciple, the one whom Jesus loved" (20:2).

In John's version the burial of Jesus was completed before sundown on Friday right after the crucifixion (19:38-42), and the tomb was not sealed with a stone. So in John's account nothing obscures the startling discovery of the empty tomb by Mary Magdalene. The action is fast paced. She runs to tell the disciples, and Peter and the Beloved Disciple run, in turn, to see the tomb.

John displays a precise knowledge of the plan and structure of first century rock-cut tombs in the Jerusalem area. The way he describes, first, the view afforded the Beloved Disciple before he entered the tomb and, then, what Peter saw when he went into the tomb corresponds very accurately to the physical layout of such tombs. In his gospel John also displays an accurate knowledge of Jerusalem and its surroundings. In fact, his gospel is a useful guidebook to the city.

It is surprising, therefore, that John is not much concerned with the tradition of the empty tomb. He is particularly interested in using this episode to demonstrate that the Beloved Disciple was a witness to the resurrection and to introduce the theme which underlies his Easter story, the theme of seeing and believing. Note that John makes it clear that Peter sees but that the Beloved Disciple sees *and believes* (20:6-7 and 20:8).

The Fourth Evangelist also adds a unique episode to his account of what happened at the tomb: the story of the appearance of the risen Christ to Mary Magdalene (20:11-18). In this incident John refers to the ascension of Christ (20:17; see also 7:39 and 14:12). But his notion of the ascension is very different from that of Luke. According to John the exaltation of Jesus begins with the crucifixion, and the resurrection is completed by the ascension. Jesus is lifted up on the cross, raised from the dead, and goes to the Father as part of a single action, one "hour." The stories of the appearance of Christ to his disciples that follow are descriptions of the appearances of the ascended, glorified Lord. Mary Magdalene interrupts the process, so to speak, and so she is commanded not to hold on to the risen Christ who is ascending to the Father (20:17).

John presents his own particular set of appearances of the risen Christ (20:19-29). The first of these is his account of the appearance to the disciples who are gathered together (20:19-23). Although an account of this appearance is a standard ingredient in the tradition, John tells it his own way. Notice how different John's version is from the description of the appearance to the Eleven in Luke 24:36-49 and Matthew 28:16-20. Matthew's account is quite rabbinical. Luke focuses on eating with the risen Christ. John, on the other hand, uses this episode to describe the experience of Pentecost (20:22). Notice, again, how different the setting is for the saying in John 20:23 from that in Matthew 16:19 and 18:18. Matthew emphasizes the binding and loosing, which were characteristic functions of the Jewish rabbi. John, in contrast, uses the term "forgive" which was more understandable to the Greek mind. So, according to John, Pentecost also is part of the Easter event. In this regard it is interesting to note that in the church in the West the principal gospel reading for Pentecost is John 20:19-23.

Only John recounts the episode of the appearance to Thomas (20:24-29). It is his way of handling the theme of doubting and disbelief which is part of the Easter tradition,[5] and it is his way of contradicting the docetic notion that the risen Christ did not have a tangible body (compare Luke 24:38-39). Primarily, however, John uses this episode to underscore his basic theme of seeing and believing. Thomas sees and believes.

John concludes this appearance story with the surprising statement, "Blessed are those who have *not* seen and yet believe" (20:29). So, according to John, Mary Magdalene, Peter and Thomas see and eventually believe. The Beloved Disciple sees and immediately believes. The members of the community for whom John composed his gospel go one step further. They believe even though they do not see. It was to make this belief possible that John wrote his gospel (see his conclusion in 20:30-31).

At a later date an epilogue was appended to John's story of the resurrection that describes the appearance of the risen Jesus to Peter and the other disciples in Galilee (21:1-25). This episode and the account of the feeding of the Five Thousand in John 6:1-14 are the only two incidents in John's gospel which are set by the Sea of Galilee.

There are two scenes in this epilogue. In the first (21:1-14) the risen Jesus makes breakfast for his disciples on the shore of the Sea of Tiberias (John's name for this body of water).

This meal is introduced by the miracle story of the great catch of fish (21:2-8). In Luke's gospel the same miracle story is used to describe the call of Peter at the beginning of Jesus' public ministry (5:1-11). Here in John's gospel it prepares the reader for the second call of Peter which follows in John 21:15-23.

The purpose of this second scene in the epilogue was to reassure the community after the deaths of Peter and the Beloved Disciple (see 21:18-23). Whoever added this appendix knew that Peter had died a martyr's death (21:18-19). The careful interpretation given to the saying of Jesus in 21:23 clearly indicates that the Beloved Disciple, too, had died.

So the epilogue is concerned less with the resurrection and more with the resurrection community. The particular community for whom John composed his gospel could well be called the community of the Beloved Disciple, who bore witness to these things (21:24).

What can we infer, then, from our examination of the distinctive features of John's story of the resurrection? First, the Fourth Evangelist used traditional material to emphasize his basic theme of seeing and believing. Peter, Mary Magdalene, and Thomas all see and subsequently believe. The Beloved Disciple sees and immediately believes. The community of the Beloved Disciple believes even though it does not see.

Second, John knows Jerusalem and he has an accurate knowledge of the type of tomb used for the burial of Jesus. He is less interested in Galilee.

Third, the community for which John writes is a community founded by the Beloved Disciple. It appears to have been somewhat separate from other communities in the early church, each of which was associated with an apostle. John goes to some length to establish the credentials of the Beloved Disciple, ranking him, in one sense, above Peter.

This was a community that was coping with the deferral of the Second Coming, a community that received the gift of the Holy Spirit, a community that did not see and yet believed. It was an all too human community. It was a church full of people like Mary Magdalene, the woman freed from seven demons who became the first witness to the risen Christ; of people like Thomas, the doubter who became the great believer. It was a community in which we could quite easily see ourselves.

We have now completed the second step in introducing you to a new approach to the gospels. Our method involves isolating each gospel account and comparing all four to discover what is distinctive in each version. The Christmas story provided us with a good way to introduce this method. The comparison of the four versions of the Easter story, however, gave us the important clues to the particular emphasis and purpose of each gospel. We can tell much about the community for which the evangelist composed his gospel by the way he told his story of the resurrection.

Mark told his Easter story to prepare a community facing catastrophe to look for the Second Coming of the risen Christ with hope. Matthew emphasized the presence of the new Moses who commissioned his followers to proclaim his new Torah to the world. Luke separated history into three epochs and stressed the eucharistic presence of the risen Christ in his church throughout the third, and present, epoch. John encouraged a community, not founded by an apostle, to persevere in their faith despite the fact that they did not see the risen Lord. He reminded them that they have the gift of the Holy Spirit and the power of forgiveness.[5]

Each of these Easter stories forms the climax of the passion narrative in that gospel. We shall turn next, therefore, to an examination of the tradition of Christ's crucifixion. The passion narrative was probably the earliest part of the gospel tradition which was organized into a fixed form. An examination of this material, then, will test our method. We shall attempt to isolate and compare the separate gospel versions of the Good Friday story in order to let each gospel speak for itself.

3

The Good Friday Stories

The preaching of Christ crucified is one of the oldest elements in the Christian gospel. It predates Paul's writings. For example, it figures prominently in the two hymns describing Christ that were mentioned in connection with John's Christmas story—Philippians 2:6-11 and Colossians 1:15-20. Philippians 2:8 says Christ was "obedient unto death, even death on a cross"; and Colossians 1:19-20 says the Christ in whom "all the fulness of God was pleased to dwell" made peace "by the blood of his cross." "That Christ died for our sins in accordance with the scriptures" is also part of the traditional gospel quoted by Paul in 1 Corinthians 15:3-7.

Paul himself made the proclamation of the word of the cross, the power of God, central to his letters. (See, for example, 1 Corinthians 1:17-18, 2:2, Galatians 6:14, and Ephesians 2:13-16.) Being buried with Christ in order to share his risen life is Paul's classic description of baptism (Romans 6:3-11), and being crucified with Christ is Paul's way of summing up Christian living (Galatians 2:20).

But the first followers of Jesus had difficulty making sense of the ignominious death of their Messiah. The preaching of Christ crucified was as Paul says, "a stumbling block to Jews and folly to Gentiles" (1 Corinthians 1:22-23). However, since the cross was at the very center of the disciples' experience, the early church had to explain the purpose of Jesus' death. One way to do this was to tell the story of his crucifixion. This is why the Good Friday story, which is customarily called the passion narrative, became the earliest part of the gospel tradition to be organized into a fixed form.

So an examination of the accounts of Jesus' death on the cross will be a test of our approach to the study of the gospels. If our method is sound, we shall discover that, despite having to use very traditional material, each evangelist managed to tell the Good Friday story in his own way. We shall begin by examining Mark's passion narrative, the earliest version of the four.

Mark's Good Friday Story

Before we can detect Mark's contributions to the passion narrative, we will have to familiarize ourselves with the traditional story of the crucifixion. It contains three acts. It begins with the account of the arrest of Jesus which includes the plot to betray him, his last supper with his disciples, and his prayers in Gethsemane followed by his arrest. The second act in the story is the account of the trial of Jesus. It includes his hearing before the Jewish authorities and his trial before Pilate. The final act in the drama is the crucifixion itself which concludes with the account of the death and burial of Jesus.

Mark is fairly faithful to the tradition. So the following outline of Mark 14 and 15 will help you identify the elements in the tradition and see the basic structure of the passion story:

1. The Arrest of Jesus (Mark 14:1-52)
   a. The anointing of Jesus (14:3-9)
   b. The plot to betray Jesus (14:10-11)
   c. The Passover meal (14:12-25)
   d. Jesus' prayer in Gethsemane (14:32-42)
   e. The arrest of Jesus in Gethsemane (14:43-52)
2. The Trial of Jesus (Mark 14:53-15:20)
   a. The night trial before the Sanhedrin (14:53, 55-65)
   b. Peter's denial of Jesus (14:54, 66-72)
   c. The morning session of the Sanhedrin (15:1)
   d. The trial before Pilate (15:2-20)
3. The Crucifixion of Jesus (Mark 15:21-47)
   a. The crucifixion and death of Jesus (15:21-39)
   b. The burial of Jesus, witnessed by the women (15:40-47)

Now that you have a clear picture of the episodes in the passion narrative, we are ready to try to discover the material Mark added to the traditional story. You will find the outline a useful map should you wish to refresh your memory about the details as we go along.

Mark makes five additions to the story of the arrest of Jesus. First, he inserts the episode of the anointing of Jesus (14:3-9). We know that this incident was originally independent of the passion narrative since Luke places it in a very different context in which the emphasis is on forgiving sinners (see Luke 7:36-50). Mark makes it clear that, for him, the anointing was for Jesus' burial (14:8).

Next Mark makes two additions to the episode of the Passover meal. He inserts a Son of man saying in 14:21. Mark identifies Jesus as the apocalyptic savior, the Son of Man, at the pivotal point in his gospel just after Peter acclaimed Jesus as the Messiah at Caesarea Philippi. The saying he introduces in 8:31 predicts that the Son of man will suffer, be killed, and rise again. Then Mark punctuates his gospel at significant points with similar predictions of the death and resurrection of the Son of man in 9:31 and 10:32-34. Now, at the supper, Mark again identifies Jesus as the Son of man. There is a further reference to the Son of man (see 14:41) in the account of Jesus' prayer in Gethsemane.[1]

Mark also underscores the apocalyptic expectation of sharing the Messianic banquet by adding the word "new" to the traditional Jewish saying in 14:25. At the end of the Passover seder, modern Jews the world over customarily say, "Next year in Jerusalem!" Mark has Jesus say, in effect, "Next year in the Kingdom of God!"

Mark adds Jesus' prediction that he will go before the disciples to Galilee after this resurrection (14:28). It is related to Mark 16:7, which forms, as we have seen, an important part of Mark's Easter story.

Finally, after the arrest of Jesus when his followers desert him, Mark alone reports than an unnamed young man ran away, naked, into the night (14:51-52). This enigmatic reference to an unknown disciple has tantalized readers ever since.

In addition to Mark's contribution to the story of the arrest, we can detect his influence in two places in the story of the trial of Jesus. In Mark's report of the night trial before the Sanhedrin (and he is the only evangelist who considers this session a trial) he has Jesus answer the High Priest's question with the final and most emphatic Son of man saying in this gospel, "You will see the Son of man seated at the right hand of Power, and coming with the clouds of heaven" (14:62).

This is doubly significant since, according to Mark, it is only here and once before Pilate (15:2) that Jesus speaks during his trials. In fact, his silence disturbs both the High Priest (14:60) and Pilate (15:5). It is clear that Pilate judges Jesus to be innocent of the charge of sedition brought against him by the Jewish leaders (see 15:10, 14). He bows, however, to the pressure from the Jewish crowd and condemns Jesus to be crucified.

Mark's insistence upon the silence and innocence of Jesus

is undoubtedly a reflection of the prophecy in Isaiah 52:13-53:12, a song of the suffering servant who, though innocent, goes silently to his death, giving his life for the guilty. (Read, particularly, Isaiah 53:7-9.) We pointed out the reference to another of these servant songs in the saying proclaimed at Jesus' baptism (see the comment on Mark 1:11 in the section of Chapter 1 on Mark's Christmas story). This anonymous Old Testament prophet became the model by which early Christians explained the purpose of Jesus' death.

Mark makes a very significant addition to the story of Jesus' crucifixion. The earliest tradition recorded that Jesus uttered a loud cry just before he died on the cross (see Mark 15:37). Mark identifies this cry as the opening verse of Psalm 22, quoted in Aramaic with its translation: "My God, my God, why hast thou forsaken me?" (15:34).

Read this psalm and you will see how well it fits these circumstances. It includes a description of a person suffering tortures similar to those brought on by crucifixion (verses 14-15) and references to mocking the victim (verses 6-8) and dividing the victim's garments (verses 16-18). This psalm soon became *the* passion psalm for Christians both because it was so appropriate and because, although it begins with a cry of despair (verses 1-2), it ends with a burst of praise to God for his deliverance (verses 22-31). This quotation from Psalm 22 has to be Mark's addition to the passion narrative since it is obvious from what follows in Mark 15:35 that what Jesus said was not clear. He may have been calling for Elijah.

These, then, are Mark's additions to the traditional passion narrative. What do they tell us about Mark's Good Friday story? Taken singly, they seem like small insertions. When we stand back, however, and look at Mark's passion narrative as a whole, we can see that he made his additions to the traditional story to emphasize the *necessity* for Jesus' death.

Jesus predicted his death (see the Son of man sayings in Mark 8:31, 9:31, and 10:32-34). He was anointed for it (14:3-9). He celebrated his death (14:22-25, particularly verse 25), and he consented to it (14:32-42). Finally, he went to his death silently, an innocent man (15:1-32). The cry that came from his lips just before he died on the cross was not a whimper of despair but a shout of praise to God in anticipation of his deliverance from death itself (15:34).

For Mark, Jesus was the perfect martyr, and his death was the perfect example for Mark's readers who were themselves facing martyrdom. Even though he had to deal with material which was fixed by tradition, Mark was able to tell the Good Friday story in his own way simply by making significant additions at critical points.

We have reviewed Mark's passion narrative in some detail and outlined the episodes in the traditional story so that you will have a standard for comparison when we examine the passion narrative in the other three gospels. We will turn next to Matthew's Good Friday story since it is so similar to Mark's.

Matthew's Good Friday Story

Matthew follows his Marcan source so faithfully in telling his Good Friday story that we can use the same outline we developed as a guide to Mark's passion narrative as a map to help you identify the episodes in Matthew 26 and 27 (see the outline earlier in this chapter). We can proceed directly, therefore, to an examination of the additions and changes Matthew makes in his version.

There are three main differences between Matthew's passion narrative and Mark's. First, Matthew adds some references to fulfilling the scriptures. According to his version, Jesus is not helpless when Judas and the crowd from the priests and Jewish elders come to arrest him (Matthew 26:53). He chooses to act in a non-violent fashion in order to fulfill the scriptures (26:54). Two other examples of Matthew's references to fulfilling the scriptures are the mention of gall in 27:34 (compare Mark's mention of myrrh in Mark 15:23) — an allusion to Psalm 69:21 — and the independent translation of the Hebrew of Psalm 22:8 in Matthew 27:43.

Then Matthew adds some traditional material about

Judas, again with scriptural allusions. Matthew 26:14-16 gives details of the plot against Jesus including the payment of the thirty pieces of silver (verse 15). Matthew's readers would recognize this as the price of a slave (see Exodus 21:32) and the wages of the shepherd "doomed to be slain for those who trafficked in the sheep," as prophesied in Zechariah 11:7 and 11:12. Matthew 27:3-10 is one tradition about the return of the money and Judas' suicide (the other is found in Acts 1:18-19). The reference in 27:9 which Matthew attributes to Jeremiah is actually found in Zechariah 11:13. But, then, the evangelists were not infallible!

All these additions are quite in keeping with Matthew's emphasis on fulfilling the scriptures, but they make little difference in the passion story.

The most important difference between Matthew's version of the Good Friday story and Mark's is the context in which Matthew places his passion narrative. In Mark the passion narrative follows directly after the great apocalyptic prediction in Mark 13. Matthew inserts a chapter (25) between the Marcan apocalypse (Matthew's version is in chapter 24) and the passion narrative (Matthew 26 and 27).

This chapter, Matthew 25, contains two parables found only in Matthew's gospel: the parable of the wise and foolish maidens (25:1-13) and the description of the last judgment (25:31-46). To these Matthew adds a parable from the sayings source used by both Matthew and Luke[2]: the parable of the talents (Matthew 25:14-30; compare Luke 19:11-27). Luke, however, uses this parable in a very different context.

Matthew 25, then, is the unique construction of this evangelist. It begins with the admonition to watch for the eschatological marriage feast (25:1-13), but it goes on to exhort those watching for the Second Coming to make responsible use of their talents while waiting (25:14-30). The judgment rests, according to Matthew, on keeping the new Torah. This is what divides the sheep from the goats.

By adding this material in Chapter 25, Matthew shifted the apocalyptic emphasis in Mark's version to an emphasis on fulfilling the law and the prophets, a characteristic theme of Matthew's gospel. He reenforced this theme by adding to his passion narrative motifs introduced in the Sermon on the Mount (Matthew 5-7). For example, in Gethsemane Jesus prays the third petition from the Lord's Prayer (26:42; compare 6:10). Jesus advocates peace at his arrest (26:52; compare 5:39). Jesus never relaxes the commandments. He is righteous (27:4,19,24; compare 5:19-20). He refuses to reply to the High Priest's request for an oath (26:63; compare 5:34). All these examples are Matthew's additions to his Marcan source. In this setting, then, Matthew's passion narrative takes on a meaning totally different from Mark's.

So Matthew found a different way of putting his stamp on the traditional passion story he inherited from Mark. He simply placed his Good Friday story in a different context.

The differences between Mark's passion narrative and Luke's version, to which we turn now, indicate that Luke, unlike Matthew, had a different source for his Good Friday story.

Luke's Good Friday Story

Even though Luke had a different source for his passion narrative (Luke 22 and 23), it followed the traditional arrangement of the arrest, trial, and crucifixion of Jesus. So Mark's passion narrative and the outline we prepared to guide you through it will still be of some help in comparing Luke's version of the Good Friday story (see the outline earlier in this chapter). Some of the differences may be due to Luke's different source, but for our purpose it will not be necessary to distinguish between these and Luke's own additions to his passion narrative. It will be sufficient for us simply to note the differences in Luke's version. This will show us how he told the Good Friday story in his own way.

The first set of significant differences is in Luke's account of the Last Supper (22:14-23). In this version, the cup comes before the bread. (See verse 17. The second half of verse 19 and verse 20 should be omitted. They do not occur in all ancient manuscripts.) This is the normal order of the Jewish sabbath meal when the kiddush, the blessing of the cup of wine, comes before the blessing of the bread. In addition, the cup (with the omission of verse 20) is not associated with the establishment of a new covenant.

So the supper in Luke's passion narrative is probably not a Passover meal but a fellowship meal much like a sabbath meal. Note the word "again" is missing from the saying in the best manuscripts of Luke 22:16 (compare Mark 14:25). In Luke's account, therefore, Jesus' desire to eat the Passover with his followers before his suffering is *not* fulfilled. Later Christians identified the Last Supper with the Passover meal. They added the word "again" to verse 16 and they also added verses 19b-20 to make Luke's account conform with the version of Mark and Matthew.

Luke's main emphasis in this episode is on a feast of anticipation. Note the term "fulfilled" in verse 16 and the slight modification of the Marcan saying in verse 18 (compare Mark 14:25). The theme in Luke's gospel is that of promise and fulfillment in history. So this last supper Jesus shares with his disciples before his crucifixion looks ahead to the suppers they will share with their risen Lord after Easter, an important element, as we have seen, in Luke's Easter story.

Luke inserts a farewell discourse in 22:24-38. Mark, who is concerned with the imminent Second Coming of the risen Christ, has no need of a farewell scene! Nor does Matthew who makes the point that the risen Jesus is present with his church to the end of the age (28:20). The ascension is an important element in Luke's Easter story, however, and he prepares for it by including this farewell discourse.

Luke adds a detail to the story of Jesus' arrest (located by Luke on the Mount of Olives). He describes Jesus' healing of the High Priest's slave, whose ear was cut off by one of Jesus' followers (22:51).

The night trial before the Sanhedrin in Mark's passion narrative becomes a preliminary hearing in Luke's version (22:54, 63-65). This is certainly more plausible, historically, since the Mishnah, part of the Jewish Talmud, prohibits a night session of the council. It is most unlikely that the Sanhedrin would have met after sundown on the night of the first Passover seder as Mark claims. Even the appearance of Jesus before the Sanhedrin the next morning is not a trial (22:66-71). In Luke's account, no charge is brought or verdict rendered in either of the two arraignments of Jesus before the Jewish authorities (compare Mark 14:64).

The only trial, therefore, in Luke's passion narrative is the trial before Pilate where the Sanhedrin brings the charge of sedition against Jesus (23:1-25). In this episode, Luke adds three statements by Pilate of Jesus' innocence (23:4, 14, 22). He also inserts the incident in 23:6-16 in which we learn that Pilate sent Jesus to Herod Antipas, hoping to avoid sentencing a man he considered innocent, and that it was Herod's soldiers, not the Roman troops, who mocked Jesus. In Luke's account of the trial the traditional motif of Jesus' innocence, the innocence of the suffering servant, now becomes a defense of the behavior of the Roman procurator and his soldiers. It was not the Romans, says Luke, but the Jews who found Jesus guilty and wanted him put to death.

Luke makes two important changes in the description of Jesus' crucifixion (23:26-56). First, he introduces two sayings which emphasize Jesus' forgiveness of sinners, an important theme in Luke's gospel. One is the familiar word from the cross: "Father, forgive them for they know not what they do" (23:34 — a saying, however, that is omitted in many ancient manuscripts). The other is Jesus' reply to the penitent thief: "Truly, I say to you, today you will be with me in paradise" (23:43). Only Luke describes one of the robbers crucified with Jesus as a repentant thief (compare Mark 15:32).

Then Luke introduces two very different sayings in place of those in Mark 15:34 and 15:39. He substitutes a quotation from Psalm 31:5, "Father, into thy hands I commit my spirit" (23:46), for the opening verse of Psalm 22, "My God, my God, why has thou foresaken me?" By so doing he radically alters the mood of the scene. Jesus does not cry out in desperation for God's deliverance, a cry which would make sense to Christians who believed they were standing on the brink of the Second Coming. Instead he entrusts himself to God's providence for the coming epoch in history when God will work out his purpose. This was a message Luke's readers would appreciate.

Luke also replaces the more familiar words of the centurion who witnessed the crucifixion and death of Jesus—"Truly, this man was a son of God."—with the statement, "Certainly, this man was innocent" (23:47). Thus Luke concludes his story of the passion with a reaffirmation of the favorable attitude the Romans showed toward Jesus.

These differences in Luke's passion narrative may seem minor, taken singly, but they all add up. Some, like his accounts of the Last Supper and the arraignment of Jesus before the Jewish authorities, make the historical record more accurate. Others, like his addition of Jesus' sayings about forgiveness and his insistence on the favorable attitude of the Romans toward Jesus, brought important messages to the church of his day. This was a church from whom the expectation of the Second Coming was far removed. It was a church that was certain it had to live in the Roman Empire for a long time.

Luke, like Mark, adapted the traditional passion story for his purposes by making small but significant additions. He probably also made use of a source more to his liking. Thus he was able to tell the Good Friday story in his own way.

We will conclude our comparison of the stories of the crucifixion with an examination of John's passion narrative. This is the Good Friday story that differs the most from Mark's version.

John's Good Friday Story

John employs all three techniques we have observed so far to modify the traditional passion story to suit his particular perspective. He places his passion narrative in a unique context. He uses a different source than Mark, and he makes additions at critical places.

In John's gospel, there is no apocalyptic preface such as

we found in Mark 13. Nor is there a description of the last judgment like the one in Matthew 25. Instead, John introduces his passion narrative with Jesus' farewell discourse (actually two discourses, one in chapter 14 and the other in 15 and 16) and his final prayer (17).

The source John uses is different from the one employed by Mark. It bears some similarity to the source Luke used. John agrees with Luke that the Last Supper is not a Passover meal (see the comments on Luke 22:14-23). In fact, he does not describe the supper at all but introduces instead an account of the foot washing (13:3-20). This is the setting for Jesus' proclamation of the new commandment: To love one another as he has loved us (13:34). Incidentally, it is this saying that gives the name to the Thursday in Holy Week, "Maundy Thursday," the day of commandment. (The Latin verb *mando* means "I command.")

Both John and Luke separate the story of Jesus' anointing from the passion narrative. John inserts it in 12:1-8 where the incident takes place six days before the Passover in Bethany, and it is Mary, the sister of Lazarus, who anoints Jesus.

Both Luke and John emphasize Pilate's reluctance to condemn Jesus. We have just observed that in Luke's version Pilate three times finds Jesus innocent and twice tries to avoid sentencing him (Luke 23:4,14,22, and 23:16, 22). When we consider John's account of the trial (18:28-19:16), we will discover that in this version Pilate makes a determined effort to pardon Jesus.[3]

Both John and Luke, in contrast to Mark and Matthew, omit all references to a Jewish trial. John describes the appearance of Jesus before the Jewish authorities as a sort of grand jury proceeding where the suspect is questioned and the decision is made to go to trial. John adds the detail that Jesus was questioned by Annas, the father-in-law of the High Priest, before he was taken to Caiaphas (18:13,19-24).

Whether or not John used the same source as Luke, it is obvious that he told the Good Friday story in his own way. He did, however, follow the traditional sequence of events:

the arrest, trial, and crucifixion of Jesus. So we shall examine his passion narrative in that order.

In John's account of the arrest (18:1-27), Jesus is in command. Although Judas, the soldiers, and the officers from the chief priests and the Pharisees come out to arrest him, Jesus takes charge. Judas need not identify him with a kiss. Jesus, "knowing all that was to befall him" (verse 4), steps forward himself. Then he identifies himself with the unequivocal declaration, "I am he" (verse 6). This is such an explicit claim to Lordship that it bowls over his accusers, and they fall to the ground.

If the impact of this saying is lost on you, you will want to review the many places in John's gospel where the evangelist places these words on Jesus' lips. It is an impressive list!

"I am the bread of life" (6:35).
"I am the light of the world" (8:12).
"I am the door of the sheep" (10:7).
"I am the good shepherd" (10:11).
"I am the resurrection and the life" (11:25).

And the most dramatic example of all is: "Before Abraham was, I am" (8:58). In Hebrew, the letters of the verb "I am" are the same as the letters of the proper name of God, "Yahweh." (This name is often translated "Jehovah" or by the title "Lord" in English versions of the Bible.) So the statement "I am" is tantamount to a claim to divinity. This is why the Jews reacted to Jesus' statement in John 8:58 by attempting to stone him to death for blasphemy. This is why it caused such consternation among those who came to arrest Jesus.

The absence of any reference to Jesus wrestling in prayer in Gethsemane in John's gospel reenforces the point that throughout his arrest Jesus is in control. (See John's version of Jesus' prayer before his passion in 12:27-28.)

In John's passion narrative, Jesus also takes command at his trial. John is probably more accurate, historically, in placing the trial and crucifixion of Jesus on the eve of the Passover (see 18:28 and 19:14). It also suits John to emphasize the point that Jesus was crucified at the precise hour in which the Passover lambs were being slaughtered. This timing echoes nicely the title given Jesus at the opening of the gospel by John the Baptist, "Behold the Lamb of God, who takes away the sin of the world!" (1:29).

John carefully describes the trial before Pilate (the only trial in John's account) in a series of seven episodes (18:28-19:16). The scene of the action alternates between the place of judgment outside the praetorium and inside the praetorium itself, that is, inside the palace. Archaeologists and historians have demonstrated that the trial of Jesus took place at the Citadel by the Jaffa Gate in Jerusalem. Originally this was a palace built by Herod the Great (one of its towers is still standing), and Roman officials stayed here when they visited Jerusalem.[4] John's description of the trial scene fits this site perfectly. Read his account of the trial to familiarize yourself with the details of this event before we focus our attention on those features which are unique to John's version.

The key words to look for in this account are "king" and "truth." Throughout John's story of the trial there are repeated references to Jesus' kingship. In 18:33, Pilate asks Jesus if the charge of sedition against him is correct, "Are you the King of the Jews?" Jesus replies that his kingship is not of this world (18:36). Pilate concludes that Jesus is a king, but Jesus says that "king" is Pilate's word (18:37). In 18:39, Pilate repeats the title when he asks the crowd if they do not want him to release the King of the Jews. The soldiers mock Jesus by hailing him as a king in 19:3. Pilate, then, presents Jesus to the Jews with the proclamation, "Behold your king!" (19:14). When they reply by demanding his crucifixion, Pilate asks again, "Shall I crucify your king?" But they answer, "We have no king but Caesar" (19:15).

John makes it clear by the way he tells the story of the trial that Jesus is a king. Of course he is not, politically speaking, the King of the Jews. But there is a certain irony in the repetition of this title. Jesus truly is a king. His kingship is not of this world, but he was born to bear witness to the truth

(18:37-38). He is the Word which "became flesh and dwelt among us, full of grace and truth" (1:14). Truth here means faithfulness, and the reference is to the faithfulness of God. He is working out his purpose in the world through Jesus.

By his description of the trial, John turns things around. The silent Jesus of Mark's version has a lot to say in this account. In John's passion narrative, it is Pilate, not Jesus, who is on trial. It is Pilate who is brought before the bar of truth. Jesus remains in control of his passion.

This is certainly true of the final event in the passion narrative, the crucifixion (19:17-42). According to John, the story of Jesus' crucifixion is the story of his enthronement. He carries his cross to Golgotha himself without any help (19:17). He is lifted up on the cross (see the prediction in 12:31-32). The familiar title tacked to his cross now takes on a new dimension. He is the king of all, and the cross is his throne. He is wearing the seamless, priestly robe of a king (see 19:23-24). John makes Jesus' crucifixion the high point of his hour of glory. When Jesus is lifted up on the cross, he is not the victim, but the victor! Even his thirst is no longer a sign of his frail humanity but evidence of his omniscience (see 19:28). Jesus' final word from the cross is a declaration of his triumph. "It is finished!" he says, which means, "I have accomplished the work I was sent to do!" (19:30).

Still in the midst of his victory Jesus has a moment to commend his mother to the care of the Beloved Disciple (19:25-27). This episode, which is unique to John's gospel, is part of this evangelist's emphasis on the role of this unnamed disciple. John uses this incident to show that Jesus provided for the founding of a community of his followers, a community identified today as the community of the Beloved Disciple.

John also adds a detail to the account of the death of Jesus, an incident not reported by any of the other evangelists (19:31-37). He records the request of the Jews that the legs of those crucified be broken to hasten their deaths since it was the eve of the day of Preparation, and he describes how the soldiers carried out this request. When they came to Jesus and saw that he had already died, one of them pierced his side with a spear to make doubly sure he was dead (verse 34). The eyewitness to this might have been the Beloved Disciple himself (verse 35).

The curious reference to the flow of blood and water from the spear wound (verse 34) is John's way of affirming that the prophecy quoted earlier in 7:38, "Out of his heart shall flow rivers of living water," has been fulfilled in Jesus' hour of glory. The addition of the blood is probably due to the insistence in the community of the Beloved Disciple that Jesus Christ came "by water and blood...not with water only but with water and blood" (see 1 John 5:6). In John 7:39, the evangelist claimed that this prophecy was a reference to the Spirit. So John must have understood this episode at the end of Jesus' crucifixion to be a sign of the giving of the Spirit as Jesus promised his disciples in his final discourse (see 14:16-17, 26, 15:26, 16:7, 13). The death of Jesus, then, becomes the beginning of the Christian life in the Spirit.

All in all, John tells a very different Good Friday story than the other evangelists. He placed his passion narrative in a different context. He used a different source, and he made significant additions to the traditional account in order to emphasize his particular perspective on the events. It is clear that John tells the Good Friday story in his own way.

We have put our approach to the study of the gospels to the test. The passion story was in a fairly fixed form before any of the evangelists composed his gospel. However, by applying our method of isolating and comparing the material in the gospels to an analysis of the passion narrative, we have demonstrated that each gospel writer was still able to tell the story in his own way. In addition, by letting each gospel speak for itself we have gained a clearer understanding of the particular message each evangelist brings us in his Good Friday story.[5]

It is time now for you to apply this approach to a more systematic investigation of the gospels. In the last chapter, therefore, I shall supply you with some directions for the study of each gospel.

4

The Gospels

The purpose of this chapter is to get you started on the right foot as you apply the method you have now learned to your own study of the gospels. It is not a commentary on the gospels nor a comprehensive guide to gospel research. For serious study you should learn to use a commentary and the other tools of the trade of biblical research. You will find a list of them in the Study Notes.[1] This chapter is designed to give some direction to your further study and provide you with a working model for applying the method to which you have been introduced.

We shall begin then with some general remarks. We have been taking some basic assumptions of biblical scholars for granted. First, the gospels are not primarily historical, but theological documents. They are proclamations in narrative form that Jesus is Lord and the Christ. So "story" is about the best word we have to describe a gospel. Each gospel tells its own story of the good news of Jesus. Remember, therefore, that each gospel is unique. This will help you ask the right questions about the biblical material.

Take the Easter story, for example. In Mark, the risen Christ does not appear at all to his disciples. In Matthew, he appears to them in Galilee. In Luke and John he appears to them in Jerusalem. The questions you will be tempted to ask are: Which of these accounts is true? Did Jesus appear to his followers after his resurrection? If so, where? But these are historical questions. The more important questions, the questions you should be asking, are theological: What is each evangelist's particular understanding of the resurrection? What is he trying to say to his readers, and to me, about the meaning of the resurrection?

Second, originally the gospels were written and circulated anonymously. Questions about the authorship of the gospels are not very important. So keep in mind that it is not who wrote the gospel but what the gospel says that counts. The earliest gospel did not appear until more than a generation after the death of Jesus, so the gospels could not have been written by contemporaries of Jesus. Since Marcus is the most common name in the Roman Empire, the author of the second gospel may well have been named Mark. It is unlikely, however, that the evangelist is the John Mark of Acts 12:12,25 or the Mark of 1 Peter 5:13. In the ancient world it was customary to assign the names of famous persons to writings to give these writings prestige. This is probably why the names of important New Testament figures like Matthew, Luke, and John got attached to those gospels. We cannot identify with certainty the author of any of the gospels, and we use the traditional designations of "Matthew," "Mark," "Luke," and "John" only for convenience.

Third, New Testament scholars have demonstrated that Mark was the first gospel to be written, and that Matthew and

Luke used Mark and a collection of sayings called Q as sources.[2] Furthermore, they have shown that Mark, Matthew, and Luke are so closely related that they have a common perspective. This is why they are called the Synoptic gospels (those that see with the same eye). Keep this in mind as you compare the material in these gospels.

Finally, each gospel, like any story, was intended to be understood as a whole. We are so accustomed to hearing, or reading, the gospels in bits and pieces that we rarely grasp the overall message of any of the evangelists. Have you ever read a gospel straight through at one sitting? This is an excellent preliminary exercise. You may want to start with Mark since it is both the earliest and the shortest gospel.

Mark's Story of the Good News of Jesus

The key to Mark's story is the structure of his gospel. He divides his proclamation of the good news of Jesus the Christ into two parts. First, there is the account of the ministry of Jesus in Galilee which is introduced by the report of his baptism by John. The turning point in Mark's story is the identification of Jesus as the Messiah by his disciples at Caesarea Philippi (8:27-9:1). Then the second half of the gospel is devoted to the passion narrative which ends abruptly with the account of the empty tomb, the astonishment and fear of the women who discover it, and the command to return to Galilee to wait for the risen Christ. Central to the structure of the second half of the gospel is chapter 13, the Marcan Apocalypse.[3] This forms the context for the entire story. Mark's gospel is an eschatological proclamation of the coming again of the risen Christ.

His portrayal of the Christ as the perfect martyr and the attention he draws to the church in "Galilee" strongly suggest he composed his gospel for a Christian community somewhere outside Palestine which was facing what looked like the end of the world.

All this you have already gleaned from the preceding

chapters. These deductions are supported by further information in the gospel. The references in Mark 13:3,14 to the temple in Jerusalem indicate that this gospel was composed before Titus destroyed the temple in A.D. 70. Moreover, it was written for gentile Christians. Mark 10:12 mentions divorce for women, which was prohibited in Palestine. There are several passages in the gospel which give evidence of ignorance of Palestinian Aramaic and Jewish customs (see, for example, 5:41; 7:3-4,11,34; 15:22). Mark describes the appearance of Jesus before the Sanhedrin at night as a trial (14:53,55-65), but the Mishnah forbids the Sanhedrin to meet after sundown.

In addition, these inferences are supported by the tradition about the gospel. The fourth-century church historian Eusebius records an early claim that this gospel came from Rome. Events in Rome in the mid-60s do provide an appropriate background for some of the major themes in Mark. Tacitus, the first-century Roman historian, records the persecution of the Christians by the Emperor Nero. It seems they took the blame for that famous fire in Rome. So Mark's message which emphasizes the inevitability of suffering for those who would follow Jesus (8:34-38; 9:33-50; 10:38-43, and 13:9-13) and his portrayal of Jesus as the perfect martyr (Mark 14 and 15) would have had special meaning for Christians in Rome during those days.

The dominant theme in Mark is the expectation of the imminent Second Coming of Christ. It grows out of the apocalyptic perspective which is characteristic of this gospel, and it too would have had a special meaning for Christians facing persecution and death. It is in the context of the expectation of the Second Coming that Mark emphasizes the necessity for Jesus' death and his willingness to accept it. It is in this context that he warns those who would follow Jesus of the cost of discipleship. The fact that Christ's Second Coming is expected momentarily lends urgency to Mark's gospel message.

Mark was not concerned with proving that Jesus is the Messiah. He took that for granted. He wanted to make clear what kind of Messiah Jesus is. But he had a problem. Why didn't Jesus disclose the fact that he was the Messiah early in his ministry? Why wasn't he recognized as the Messiah right away by his disciples? To solve this problem Mark treated Jesus' identity as a secret for the first half of his gospel. In the beginning only the demons (1:24,34; 3:11-12) and those who are healed (1:44, 5:43, 7:36, 8:26) recognize Jesus as the Messiah. It wasn't until the disciples were prepared to go with Jesus to Jerusalem that they recognized his true identity (8:27-30). So the "messianic secret" is a constant theme in the first part of Mark's gospel.

Mark's story moves rapidly. One of his favorite words is "immediately." He is concerned more with what Jesus did than with what Jesus said. The passion narrative makes up most of the second part. There are sixteen miracle stories in Mark, thirteen of which occur in Mark 1:16-8:21. He uses these miracle stories to proclaim Jesus' opposition to his enemies and to demonstrate the power of the Spirit working through Jesus.

Jesus confronts the demons when he drives an unclean spirit out of a man in the synagogue at Capernaum (1:23-27) and when he exorcises the Gedarene demoniac (5:1-20). He confronts sickness and death by curing a leper (1:40-45), exorcising the demon in the daughter of the Syrophoenician woman (7:25-30), stopping the hemorrhage of the woman who touched the hem of his garment, and raising the daughter of Jairus from death (5:22-43). Jesus confronts the Pharisees when he heals a paralytic (2:1-12) and a man with a withered hand (3:1-6) on the sabbath.

More important to Mark, Jesus manifests eschatological signs by stilling the storm (4:35-44), feeding the multitude (6:30-44 and 8:1-10), and curing the deaf and dumb man (7:31-37). When we compare these miracle stories in Mark with the parallel passages in Matthew and Luke we discover that Mark was using them to stress the tremendous power at work in and through Jesus. An example will illustrate this.

We'll compare the exorcism of the Gedarene demoniac in Mark 5:1-20 with the parallel versions of the story in Matthew 8:28-34 and Luke 8:26-39.

This miracle is the second of three acts of divine power

in this section of Mark's gospel. The miracle stresses the tremendous power of Jesus over demons. The miracle story itself is in verses 1-15. Verse 15 is a typical conclusion to a healing story. The popular story of a Jewish exorcism in a foreign land is a later addition to the original miracle story. In Mark this miracle takes place outside Galilee in gentile territory, and Mark makes it the inauguration of a ministry to the Decapolis (see verses 18-20). He links this story to what follows on the other side of the Sea of Galilee by inserting verses 16 and 17.

When we compare Mark's version of this story with the account in Matthew 8:28-34, we discover that Matthew reduces Mark's twenty verses to seven. He omits the details in Mark 5:3-5 and 15b-16. He also omits the reference to the mission to the Decapolis in Mark 5:18-20. He seems more concerned with the request to Jesus to leave the neighborhood, and he concludes his account on this note (Matthew 8:34). This miracle story is one of ten that Matthew selects from Mark and groups together in Matthew 8 and 9. Just as the ten plagues were signs in the time of Moses, so the ten miracles are signs in the time of Jesus, the new Moses.

Luke's version of this miracle story (8:26-39) is somewhat closer to Mark's account. But in Luke (8:27) the man with the demons comes from the city, not the tombs. There is no reference to the Decapolis in Luke's account. When the man is restored to sanity, he proclaims how much Jesus has done for him "throughout the whole city" (8:39). In Luke's gospel Jesus does not go outside Jewish territory.

From our comparison of the different versions of this story we can see that Mark's account with its vivid details heightens the miracle and emphasizes the power of Jesus. Mark alone has an interest in the mission of Jesus to the gentiles.

By contrast, Matthew's version of the story is tame. He has no interest in a mission to the gentiles, but instead he uses this miracle story to help make up a list of the ten signs of the new Moses, Jesus. Luke's account is more like Mark's but he puts it in a section of his gospel dealing with Jesus' acts rather than the outpouring of the Spirit.

These conclusions are reenforced by a comparision of several of the miracles found in Mark with the parallel versions of these stories in the other gospels. Detailed instructions for such an exercise are provided in the Study Notes, should you wish to pursue this investigation.[4]

What emerges from our consideration of the unique aspects of Mark's gospel is a paradigm, a model, for applying the approach to the study of the gospels that we have proposed. It is very simple:

1. Outline the structure of the gospel.
2. Identify the dominant themes of the gospel.
3. Distinguish the work of the evangelist from the sources he used.

By viewing each gospel as a unique composition and by looking at it as a whole, you will be able to see the purpose of the evangelist and the basic features of his "portrait" of Jesus. You can do this by outlining the structure of the gospel. This will also help you to identify the major themes in the evangelist's story. By isolating significant passages in one gospel and comparing them with parallel passages in the other gospels, and by noting the context of the passage in each gospel you will gradually develop the ability to recognize each evangelist's handiwork and separate it from the sources he used.

The last step is more difficult in Mark than in the other gospels, since Mark was the first to use the gospel form. It is easier to see what Matthew and Luke did with the material from Mark that they used. Still a comparison of material in Mark with the parallel passages in Matthew and Luke, such as the comparison of the miracle stories, tells us in reverse, so to speak, a lot about Mark's style and purpose. The uniqueness of the structure of Mark's gospel is emphasized by comparing it with the very different structure of John's gospel.

I'll use this paradigm to suggest a direction for your study of the other gospels, beginning with Matthew.

Matthew's Story of the Good News of Jesus

Matthew organized the material he used to tell his gospel story in a deliberate and systematic way. On the surface, it looks as if he followed the structure he inherited from Mark by dividing his gospel into two parts. Each of these sections begins with the phrase "from the time that Jesus began" (Matthew 4:17 and 16:21). In the first part Matthew recounts the ministry of Jesus in Galilee and in the second he deals with his ministry in Jerusalem. Matthew introduces the whole story with his version of the birth narrative (1 and 2) plus the account of the baptism and temptation of Jesus (3:1-4:16), and he concludes it with the passion and resurrection narratives (26-28).

However, a closer inspection of the gospel reveals a more elaborate structure. The birth story and the passion and resurrection narratives surround a carefully organized set of five units of material beginning with chapter 3. Each unit is marked off by the editorial phrase "when Jesus had finished" (see 7:28, 11:1, 13:53, 19:1 and 26:1). Each unit, in turn, is divided into a narrative and a teaching section. Matthew deliberately organized his gospel in imitation of the five books of Moses, the Torah (the first five books of the Old Testament).

You have already discovered in the preceding chapters that Matthew presents Jesus as the new Moses who recapitulates Israel's experiences of the Exodus and the Exile. You have just learned from our examination of the miracle stories in Mark that Matthew strengthens this identification of Jesus with Moses by listing the ten signs he performed (Matthew 8-9). It follows then that this new Moses whose life and teachings fulfill the prophets will proclaim the new Torah, the new law.

In Matthew's gospel the teachings of Jesus overshadow his actions. He is no longer the miracle worker and martyr of Mark's gospel story but the rabbi and scribe who proclaims a higher righteousness, more demanding than the righteousness of the scribes and Pharisees.

Each of these units of material, or "books," focuses on an important theme in Matthew's gospel story. The first (3:1-7:29) contains the well-known Sermon on the Mount, Matthew's version of the new Torah. The second (8:1-11:1) deals with true discipleship. The third (11:2-13:52) concentrates on the kingdom of heaven. In the fourth "book" (13:53-19:2) Matthew describes the function of the church as a forgiving community, and in the fifth unit (19:3-26:1) he presents his view of the final judgment, which will be based on obedience to the new Torah. Obedience, in fact, is the word that best summarizes Matthew's story. Jesus himself is obedient to the new law and so fulfills the prophets. His followers in the church are called to a new, radical obedience. Matthew wrote his gospel to guide the church, and it has always had a special appeal for the church. This is probably why it was placed first in the New Testament.

As noted in the preceding chapters, Matthew composed his gospel for a Jewish-Christian congregation that was beginning to accept gentile converts. His gospel was written after the destruction of the temple in A.D. 70. His addition to the parable of the marriage feast — "The king was angry, and he sent his troops and destroyed those murderers and burned their city" (22:7; compare Luke 14:21) — probably refers to that destruction.

Matthew composed his gospel for a Jewish-Christian community — scholars say probably in Syria, possibly in Antioch — which was facing the problems of organization, the effects of separation from Judaism, and the disappointment of the eschatological hope due to the deferral of the Second Coming of Christ.

So the urgency of Mark's message and his promise of the immediate return of the risen Christ have now given way to a message designed to help Christians in the church live out their obedience to the teachings of their Lord in this world. Matthew promises them that God will always be with them. Remember that Matthew begins his gospel story by giving the name of Emmanuel, God-with-us, to Jesus at his birth and concludes it with the promise of the risen Jesus to be with his church to the end of the age. For Matthew, Jesus replaces the Jewish concept of the *shekinah,* the symbol of the presence of the unseen God in the midst of the world. Matthew also shifts the context for the passion narrative from Mark's apocalyptic setting to one in which obedience to the new Torah determines the last judgment when it finally comes.

The new law that Jesus, the new Moses, proclaims is more demanding than the Jewish Torah. In Matthew's gospel, Pharisees who in fact were scrupulous about observing the law are castigated for the hypocritical way they keep the law (see Matthew 23, for example). The Pharisees are singled out partly because they were the only sect of Judaism to survive the catastrophe of the destruction of the temple in A.D. 70. But they are condemned also because the Christian community for which Matthew wrote his gospel was struggling to establish an identity separate from that of the rabbinic Judaism that was emerging after 70.

To illustrate this, let's take a closer look at Matthew's version of Jesus' proclamation of the new law, the famous Sermon on the Mount (Matthew 5-7). Matthew depended heavily on Mark as the source for his narrative sections, but for much of the teaching material he made use of the sayings source called Q. Since Luke also used this sayings source, a comparision of Matthew's use of the sayings with that of Luke will enable us to see the particular emphasis Matthew placed on Jesus' teaching.

The so-called Sermon on the Mount is a good example of this. Strictly speaking, it is not a sermon. It is not an account of a historical event, a sermon delivered by Jesus, but a literary device of the evangelist. Matthew composed the sermon. He grouped together many teachings of Jesus to give the effect of a continous proclamation of the new Torah. The fact that these sayings of Jesus are found in different places in Luke's gospel is evidence that originally they were separate and independent.

The key to the Sermon on the Mount is the demand for

a higher righteousness in Matthew 5:17-20. It begins with Matthew's insistence that Jesus came to fulfill the law and the prophets, and it concludes with the solemn warning that unless the righteousness of the Christians exceeds that of the scribes and Pharisees they will never enter the kingdom of heaven. This is followed by a series of six antitheses between the old Torah, the Jewish law, and the new Torah proclaimed on the mount by the new Moses, Jesus (5:21-47). The chapter ends with a radical demand for obedience: "You, therefore, must be perfect, as your heavenly Father is perfect" (5:48).

With this in mind, we'll compare Matthew's version of the beatitudes (5:1-12) with those in Luke (6:17, 20-26). Matthew sets the scene for Jesus' proclamation "on the mountain," just as he placed the enthronement of the risen Jesus on "the mountain" in Galilee (Matthew 28:16). This is an obvious imitation of the giving of the law to Moses on the mountain in Sinai. In Luke the event takes place "on a level place," that is, on the plain (6:17) after Jesus came down from the mountain.

The version of the beatitudes in Luke is simpler than that in Matthew and probably closer to the original in the sayings source Q. There are fewer beatitudes in Luke, which contains no mention of the meek, the merciful, the pure in heart, or the peacemakers, but Luke adds four "woes." The promise in Luke that those who weep now will laugh (Luke 6:21) is more direct and vivid than the reference to comforting those who mourn in Matthew (Matthew 5:4).

Matthew changes the reference to the poor in Luke (Luke 6:20) to a reference to the "poor in spirit" (Matthew 5:3). He also turns those "that hunger now" (Luke 6:21) into "those who hunger and thirst after righteousness" (Matthew 5:6). The rule of thumb in comparing passages is that the simpler version is more likely to be the original one. So Matthew adapts Jesus' saying about the poor and hungry to suit his emphasis on Jesus' demand for obedience to the new Torah. The saying is no longer addressed to those who are literally poor and hungry but to the pious ones (the "poor" in Isaiah 61:1, a passage echoed in Matthew 11:5) who are thirsty for a new righteousness.

This is an example of how Matthew puts his own stamp on the teachings of Jesus—by organizing them into a unique composition, the "sermon," by locating this proclamation "on the mountain," and by adapting them to his theme of the higher righteousness. In the Study Notes you will find instructions for carrying on this comparison of Matthew's use of the sayings of Jesus in Matthew 5-7 with Luke's version of these same sayings.[5]

By using the paradigm I have attempted to get you started in the right direction for further study of Matthew's gospel story. A grasp of the outline of this gospel is fundamental to an understanding of the evangelist's message.

It is so carefully organized that the structure also reveals the important themes in this gospel.

Since the teachings of Jesus dominate Matthew's story, further comparison of the way Matthew uses the sayings of Jesus with the way Luke employs them is indicated. By continuing the comparison we began with the beatitudes you will gradually develop an awareness of Matthew's style and become more skillfull at distinguishing his work from his source material.

Next, I'll apply the paradigm to Luke's gospel.

Luke's Story of the Good News of Jesus

The structure of Luke's gospel is far less complicated than Matthew's scheme of organization. In general, Luke follows Mark's outline of the story, dividing his gospel into an account of the gathering of witnesses to Jesus in Galilee (3:1-9:50) and the story of the witness to the passion and resurrection of Jesus in Jerusalem (19:28-24:53). In between these sections he inserts a large block of material containing for the most part teachings of Jesus (9:51-19:27). Luke presents this material ostensibly as an account of the journey from Galilee to Jerusalem. However, like Matthew's Sermon on the Mount, this is a literary device by which the evangelist introduces a great many of Jesus' sayings. This is Luke's version of the witness to the word proclaimed by Jesus. Witness, then, is the term that best characterizes Luke's gospel and all who read it are called to be "witnesses of these things" (24:48).

There is no conclusion to the story in the gospel itself. That comes in Acts which is the second volume in the evangelist's work. It tells the story of the spread of the good news from Jerusalem to Rome that Jesus is the savior of the world. When the evangelist completed Acts, he added a prologue to his gospel (1:5-2:52) which gives the whole story a universal setting.

This anonymous author we call Luke was a Greek-speaking gentile Christian. His writing is more polished than that of the other evangelists, and he follows the literary conventions of his day. He is the only evangelist who tells us why he composed his gospel. Each part of his two volume work is introduced by a preface addressed to his patron Theophilus (Luke 1:1-4 and Acts 1:1-5). As he says in his preface to the gospel, his aim was to write "an orderly account" of those events witnessed first by Jesus' contemporaries and then proclaimed by the preaching of the church. He sees himself as a member of a third generation of witnesses to the good news of the salvation of the world.

Luke comes closest of all the evangelists to being what we would call a historian. He is concerned about telling the story as accurately and as completely as possible. So he uses as many sources as he can. Like Matthew, he employs Mark and Q as his basic sources, but he is much more selective than Matthew in his use of material from Mark. While Matthew incorporates most of Mark's gospel into his story, Luke uses only fifty percent of it. A good half of Luke's gospel comes from his own sources or knowledge of the tradition.

Luke begins his gospel story proper with a catalogue of Roman officials, local rulers, and Jewish high priests (3:1-2). He introduces his account of Jesus' birth with references to the governor of Syria and the Roman emperor whose decree made it necessary for Mary and Joseph to travel to Bethlehem (2:1-2). This is clear evidence of his insistence that this story takes place on the center stage of history. As we noted in the preceding chapter, Luke's attempts to straighten out some of the historical inaccuracies in Mark's passion narrative and to absolve the Roman procurator and his soldiers from blame in the crucifixion of Jesus are further evidence that this evangelist was writing for gentile Christians living somewhere in the Roman empire.

Luke and the congregation for whom he composed his gospel were fairly far removed from the events in Palestine, both in time and distance. Luke's account of Jerusalem surrounded by armies who had cast up a seige wall (Luke 21:20 and 19:43) is too accurate a description of the fall of Jerusalem to have been written before A.D. 70. His imprecise knowledge of the geography of the land and of the streets of Jerusalem indicates that for him and his readers the meaning of the land and Jerusalem was largely symbolic. For them, as for many modern Christians who have never been to Israel, it was the Bible-picture-book Holy Land.

Luke divided history into three epochs: the epoch of Israel, which ended with John the Baptist (see 16:16); the epoch of Jesus, when the good news of God was first preached and which concluded with the Ascension (Luke 24:50-52 and Acts 1:6-11); and the epoch of the church, in which his readers and we live. He composed his gospel for a church which had long since ceased to wait expectantly for the Second Coming. Luke offered this church the challenge of a worldwide mission, the reassurance of God's unlimited forgiveness, and the promise of "knowing" the risen Lord "in the breaking of the bread." These are the main themes of his message which speaks to us today as strongly as it did to those first-century Christians for whom he composed his gospel.

In the second section of his gospel, the journey to Jerusalem (9:51-19:27), Luke added some of the most famous and best loved parables to his account of the teachings of Jesus. We are accustomed to reading these, and indeed all the parables in the gospels, in the context in which the evangelist set them. It may surprise you therefore to discover that the parables may have been much more provocative when Jesus told them.

In the library of ancient manuscripts found at Nag Hammadi in Egypt in 1945, a collection of sayings of Jesus, called the Gospel of Thomas, was discovered.[6] Among other teachings purported to be from Jesus, this manuscript contains twelve parables which are also found in the four gospels—including a version of the parable of the rich fool in Luke 12:16-21 (Gospel of Thomas 63). The parables in the Gospel of Thomas are given little or no interpretation.

Here are two of these parables which have no parallel in the four gospels. They will illustrate just how enigmatic Jesus' teaching was for those who heard it for the first time. One parable is:

> (97) Jesus said, "The Kingdom of the [Father] is like a certain woman who was carrying a jar full of meal. While she was walking [on] a road, still some distance from home, the handle of the jar broke, and the meal emptied out behind her on the road. She did not realize it; she had noticed no accident. When she reached her house, she set the jar down and found it empty."

Immediately following is this parable:

> (98) Jesus said, "The kingdom of the Father is like a certain man who wanted to kill a powerful man. In his own house he drew his sword and stuck it into the wall in order to find out whether his hand could carry through. Then he slew the powerful man."[7]

Whether or not these are genuine sayings of Jesus is not important here. The point is that each of these parables ends abruptly without any explanation of the story. You can almost hear Jesus saying, "Let him who has ears hear." Nor does the context give us any clue. We may speculate all we please but we are still left up in the air as to the meaning Jesus gave these parables. This strongly suggests that both the church and the evangelists added interpretations to the parables we find in the gospels.

Since Luke characteristically uses material from sources known only to him, a study of the parables he adds to his gospel will help identify his style and purpose. Let's look at two examples.

First, we'll examine the parable of the rich fool in Luke 12:16-21 since we can compare it with the version of this story in the Gospel of Thomas (63). Here is the parable as it appears in that source:

> (63) Jesus said, "There was a rich man who had much money. He said, 'I shall put my money to use so that I may sow, reap, plant and fill my storehouse with produce, with the result that I shall lack nothing.' Such were his intentions, but that same night he died. Let him who has ears hear."[8]

When we compare this to Luke's version of the parable, two important points emerge. First, the emphasis in Luke's version is on the foolishness of the rich man (12:19-20), and the evangelist adds a moral at the end of the story (12:21). Second, Luke places this parable in a passage dealing with the danger of covetousness (see 12:13-15). In the Gospel of Thomas, on the other hand, this parable is simply a warning to those who would heap up possessions of the uncertainty and transitoriness of life. Luke has given this story a new twist.

This comparison is a good illustration of the importance of the way an evangelist introduces and concludes a parable and of the context in which he places it. These are the clues to the meaning he gives the parable and the purpose for which he incorporates it into his gospel.

For our second example, we'll look at the familiar parable of the good Samaritan (Luke 10:29-37). First, notice that Luke uses this parable to answer the lawyer's question, Who is my neighbor? It is Luke's commentary on the test to which Jesus was put by one of the scribes, according to Mark's gospel (12:28-34). Matthew, who also records this incident (22:34-40), concludes his account with what is for him a characteristic declaration that the two great commandments form the basis of the law and the prophets. Only Luke explores the meaning of neighbor and adds the parable of the good Samaritan.

The story is well chosen and carefully told to make Luke's point. The lawyer's question presupposes an objective definition of neighbor which by its very nature would be limiting. In the conclusion to the parable Jesus turns the question around and asks, Which one *acted neighborly* to the man who was robbed? Jesus rephrases the question so that it demands a subjective answer which is not limiting, one based on the interior motive for acting toward others. Luke appears to be emphasizing a shift in the focus of the moral demands from the external commandments to the internal motive for keeping them.

Some of the other parables that Luke alone includes in his gospel story seem to be concerned primarily with attitudes and motives, for example, the prodigal son (15:11-32), the rich man and Lazarus (16:19-31), and the Pharisee and the publican (18:9-14). The Study Notes contain instructions for a study of these and all the parables in the gospels, should you wish to pursue this investigation.[9]

Again, by using the paradigm I have tried to give direction to your further study of Luke's gospel. The special sources and material Luke used to compose his story provide us with some important clues to the unique message he proclaims. So a study of the material found only in Luke, such as the famous parables mentioned above, will help you become more familiar with his style and better able to distinguish his work from his sources.

Finally, then, I'll apply the paradigm to John's gospel.

John's Story of the Good News of Jesus

The structure of John's gospel is very different from that of the first three gospels. Although the Fourth Evangelist follows what certainly was the broad outline of Jesus' life, he does not restrict Jesus' visits to Jerusalem during his public ministry to the final trip to his death on the cross as do the Synoptic gospels, following Mark's lead.

John introduces his gospel with a prologue praising the incarnate Word (1:1-18 — the Christmas story we examined in Chapter 1). A disciple added an epilogue to the story, describing the appearance of the risen Jesus to Peter and the other disciples in Galilee (21 — see the discussion of John's Easter story in chapter 2).

The rest of the material in the gospel is divided into two sections. The climax of John's story is the one hour of glory when Jesus is lifted up on the cross, raised from the dead, and then goes to the Father. So the second half of the gospel begins with the account of the Last Supper and the final discourse (13:1-17:26) and concludes with the passion narrative (chapter 18 and 19) and the Easter story (chapter 20).

The structure of the first half of the gospel is unique. John had access to sources not known to the other evangelists. Some of the traditional material he used had been shaped into teaching, or preaching, units usually consisting of a "sign" (a miracle story) and a discourse. The Fourth Evangelist composed these units into a "Book of Signs" (1:19-12:50).

These discourses elaborate the significance of an elemental symbol suggested by the sign — symbols like bread, water, light, and life itself. In the major part of this section (5:1-10:42) these units are related to principal Jewish feasts.

John's gospel is the result of a profound reflection on the uniqueness of the relationship between Jesus and God. The influence of the Jewish wisdom movement is apparent in the designation of Jesus as the pre-incarnate Word, the bringer of light and truth to the world. In the gospel this reflection is more often expressed symbolically than historically. Although the Fourth Gospel does provide us with important historical material, and can still serve as a reliable guide to Jerusalem for the modern pilgrim, the evangelist prefers to acclaim Jesus as the lamb of God, the bread of life, the light of the world, the source of living water, the resurrection and the life. If Mark's "painting" of Jesus the martyr is in the style of Grünewald, then John's "portrait" of the incarnate Word is an El Greco.

The Fourth Evangelist addressed his message to Christian believers both gentile and Jewish. He composed his gospel to encourage them to believe, even if they did not see (20:29). The founder of this community may well have been the Beloved Disciple. He is not known to the other evangelists, but in this gospel he is given a place of honor above that of Peter. He may, in addition, have been responsible for shaping the raw material of the tradition into the teaching units used by the evangelist in his composition.

This gospel reflects the struggle for identity which was going on in the church after A.D. 70 and particularly after the expulsion of the Christians from the Jewish synagogues that took place between 80 and 90. The Fourth Evangelist used his gospel to make a case for the Christian community against the sect of John the Baptist, against Christian heretics, and especially against the Jews.

Since the first section of the gospel is unique, a study of the teaching units and the way the evangelist used them will help you discover more about John's style and purpose. Let's examine, for example, the unit of material in John 6.

This chapter is part of the series of units in which the evangelist related the teaching of Jesus to some principal Jewish feasts—to the sabbath (John 5), to the feast of Tabernacles or *Succoth* (John 7, 8, and 9), to the feast of the Dedication or *Hanukkah* (John 10), and in the passage we are examining (John 6) to the Passover.

The sign with which the unit begins is the miracle of the feeding of the five thousand (6:1-15), which John alone places at the season of the Passover (6:4). This is the only miracle story that appears in all four gospels (see Mark 6:32-44, Matthew 14:13-21, and Luke 9:10-17, as well as the variant form of this story in Mark 8:1-10 and Matthew 15:32-39). The popularity of this miracle story attests to its importance in the tradition. John uses it for a special purpose, to introduce the theme of the bread with which God feeds his faithful people.

It is interesting to note that by the time John chose to use this miracle story it had been wedded in the tradition to another miracle story, the account of Jesus walking on the sea (6:16-22). We know these stories were originally separate because Luke does not include this account of Jesus walking on the water when he records the miracle of the feeding of the multitude. But in the form in which John received the stories they are inseparable, and although this second miracle story has no place in his scheme for this chapter he is forced to include it.

John chose this miracle story precisely because it was the most appropriate sign to introduce the discourse on Jesus, the bread of life (6:25-71). John 6:25-27 connects the discourse with the conclusion of the miracle story and forms a preface to the teaching that follows. The Passover setting of the sign prepares for the reference to God's gift of manna to the Israelites during their wilderness wandering (6:31). Jesus points out that it was not Moses who gave them the manna, but God who gives the true bread from heaven (6:32). When his hearers ask for this bread Jesus states unequivocally, "I am the bread of life" (6:35). The Jews object because Jesus identifies himself as the bread that came down from heaven (6:41-42).

Two meanings are given in the discourse to the designation of Jesus as the bread of life. First, the symbol of bread is taken to signify the word of God revealed in Jesus (6:43-50). Second, bread signifies the eucharistic food, the body of Christ (6:51). This identification provokes a dispute among the Jews (6:52), which Jesus silences with his further instruction on the Eucharist (6:53-58). Following this public teaching, Jesus concludes the discourse with private instructions to his disciples (6:60-71).

The sign of this discourse, the symbol of the bread from heaven, is an important element in John's gospel story. The theme of Jesus as the bread of life, both as word and sacrament, undoubtedly had a special meaning for the community to which the evangelist wanted to give encouragement. The historical background of the chapter, its place in the ministry of Jesus, is immaterial. It could have happened anywhere at any time. The miracle story was chosen simply to introduce the symbol of the true bread.

The historical context in which the evangelist proclaimed his story is important, however. The community for which he wrote was facing a struggle with the Jews who had expelled them from their synagogues. John boldly proclaims a Christian Passover teaching which supersedes that of the Jews. He even sets the triumph of Jesus' teaching over that of the Jews *in the synagogue* at Capernaum (6:59).

The antagonism between Christians and Jews is quite apparent in these chapters. Jesus accuses the Jews of failing to keep the law (7:19). They seek to kill him (7:19,25-26). Yet Jesus, speaking openly, confounds the Jews at every turn. In the end they are confused and bewildered by his message (7:35-36).

The references to "the Jews" in these passages, and for the most part in John's gospel, are to the Jewish authorities. When John wants to praise the common people he uses the term "Israelite" (see 2:47).

After the destruction of the temple in A.D. 70 the Jews were forced to find a new focus for their religious life and a new identity. In the process Christians, most of whom were Jews, were expelled from the synagogues. So they, too, were forced to redefine their identity apart from Judaism and to discover a sense of community of their own. It is in the context of these troubled times that we must try to understand the case John makes in his gospel against the Jewish authorities.

The significance of the historical context in which John proclaimed his gospel story is a reminder to us that we must learn to read the gospels on two levels. On one level, each evangelist tells the story of Jesus' life and ministry in order to proclaim him as the Christ. On the other level, the evangelist addresses a message to the church of his day, and this level of meaning is generally the more important one. It is usually the key to the reason why the evangelist composed his gospel.

Further study of other teaching units in the first half of John's gospel will help you become more familiar with his style and the message of his gospel story. In addition to the units that relate the teaching of Jesus to Jewish feasts (5:1-10:42), there is a discourse with Nicodemus on baptism (John 3), a conversation with a Samaritan woman about the source of living water (John 4), and an instruction on resurrection at the death of Lazarus (John 11). There are directions in the Study Notes for carrying out an investigation of this material, should you wish to pursue this line of study.[10]

I have presented a paradigm to help you apply the method of study of the gospels to which I introduced you. Simply outline the structure of the gospel. Then identify the dominant themes of the gospel and, finally, begin to distinguish the work of the evangelist from the sources he used by investigating significant passages in his gospel. To get you started I have provided you with an outline and a list of the major themes for each gospel. To assist you in the last step and to whet your appetite for further study of the gospels, I have suggested some avenues you can explore. You now have all the tools necessary to let each gospel speak for itself.[11]

Two questions remain to be answered: Why did the church include all four gospels, and only these four gospels, in the final form of its scriptures? And how should these four different accounts be used to proclaim the church's single message of the good news of Christ? In the conclusion that follows, we shall address these questions by letting the church speak for itself.

Conclusion

By the end of the first century all four gospels had been written, and by the end of the second century these four gospels, and only these, were considered authentic by the church. We know very little, however, about the circumstances in which they were collected and selected by the early church.

Ignatius, who died at the beginning of the second century, probably knew Mark. He may also have known John's gospel. Justin Martyr, who lived past the middle of the second century, knew the Synoptic gospels.

Most likely, local congregations used only one gospel in the beginning. The second-century list of New Testament writings of Marcion, for example, contains only one gospel. It is also clear that there were more than four gospels in use. As they were circulated and collected, however, a process of selection took place. Some were discarded; others were recognized as authentic representations of the church's experience of Christ. By the end of the second century the list of the gospels recognized as authentic throughout the church had been narrowed down to the four we know.

The plurality of the gospels was a problem for the early church. The problem was not so much the differences between the gospels as the tendency on the part of factions in the church to adopt one gospel and exclude the others. The Judaizers in the church chose Matthew. Marcion, who wanted to rid Christianity of everything Jewish, used Luke. Those who rejected the true humanity of Jesus adapted Mark to suit their purpose, and early gnostics favored John.

At the end of the second century, however, the Christian apologist Irenaeus made a strong case justifying the use of all four gospels. From that time on, these four gospels, and only these, have been part of the church's canon of scripture, that is, the norm or rule for faith and life.

It is evident, therefore, that the early church intended to let each gospel speak for itself *as long as all four gospels were given a hearing.* Where then did the habit of harmonizing the gospels originate?

This too started in the second century when the Christian scholar Tatian produced his *Diatesseron,* the first harmony of the gospels. He skillfully wove together verses from all four gospels to produce a single story of Jesus. He omitted the genealogies in Matthew and Luke, the story of the woman taken in adultery in John, and the preamble to Luke's gospel. He included the units of material unique to Mark's gospel, but he eliminated from them the evangelist's connecting phrases. He also included all the vivid details in Mark in telling the miracle stories. Apparently he preferred the order of events in John's gospel, but he took great liberty in fitting all the incidents in Jesus' life and ministry into a single, coherent account.[1]

The influence of Tatian's harmony of the four gospels was far reaching. It became immensely popular, and it was quickly translated into the different languages used in the various parts of the church at that time. It has directly influenced the structure of all the harmonies of the gospels from the Byzantine period until modern times.

The indirect effect of Tatian's work was even greater. It became the basis of regarding the harmonized gospel account as historically trustworthy both in sequence and in content from the second century to the present day. Passion plays and preaching on "The Seven Last Words," Nativity pageants, and Christmas creches are all based on this approach to the gospels. Most so-called lives of Jesus, as well as films on the life of Christ of the Cecil B. DeMille genre, owe their form to Tatian. There are, by contrast, some contemporary studies of Jesus with a different perspective.[2] Handel's famous oratorio *The Messiah* is based on a harmonized text of the Bible. Bach, on the other hand, stuck to *St. Matthew's Passion.*

There is no doubt that the influence of Tatian has been pervasive. One fifth-century bishop considered it pernicious, and he went about destroying every copy of the *Diatesseron* he could lay his hands on. He removed two hundred copies from parishes in his diocese and replaced them with copies of the four gospels. Such drastic action may not be called for today, but there is a need for a radical change in our parishes in the approach to the gospels by laity and clergy alike.

We can take our cue from the way the gospels are read according to the eucharistic lectionary being used, with modifications, by many English-speaking churches today. This scheme of assigned scripture readings throughout the year for the liturgy was adopted by the Roman Catholic church after the Second Vatican Council, and it has become the basis of a process of ecumenical cooperation and revision facilitated by the Consultation on Common Texts, a process designed to lead to a common set of Sunday Bible readings for all the churches.

This new lectionary is based on the ancient principle of "course reading," that is, the systematic reading, week by week, of the books of the Bible in the regular worship services, and the foundation of this lectionary is the course reading of the gospels. John's gospel is read in Lent and the Easter season (plus certain other occasions). The Synoptic gospels—Matthew, Mark, and Luke—are read in turn in a three-year cycle throughout the rest of the year (except for special days or seasons).

Preachers who base their homilies on the Sunday gospel

are now forced to plan ahead! They must prepare sermons that take into account the context of the Sunday gospel reading and the continuity of the story. Religious educators are now challenged to develop courses and lesson material that fit into this new approach. All of us should adopt the practice of course reading in our private study of the gospels. We must get into the habit of reading each of the gospels systematically, from beginning to end, the same way we read any story.

It is time to rediscover the creative genius of each evangelist. Instead of trying to harmonize the gospels, we should emphasize the differences between them. This will help us see the distinctive features of the portrait of Jesus each gospel writer paints and open our ears to hear his particular message. It is time to let each gospel speak for itself.

STUDY NOTES

Introduction

1. Redaction Criticism

The technical term for the approach to the study of the gospels presented in this book is redaction criticism. Hans Conzelmann, Günther Bornkamm, and Willi Marxsen were the first to apply this method to the Synoptic gospels. More recently, J. Louis Martyn and Raymond E. Brown have been influenced by this approach in their studies of John's gospel.

Redaction criticism is the accepted English translation of the German word *redaktionsgeschichte*. "It is concerned," as Norman Perrin says, "with studying the theological motivation of an author as this is revealed in the collection, arrangement, editing and modification of traditional material, and in the composition of new material or the creation of new forms within the traditions of early Christianity" *(What Is Redaction Criticism?,* p.1). It would be just as appropriate to call it composition criticism since it takes seriously the creative work of an author who puts together material from traditional sources to create his own distinctive composition.

Redaction criticism developed after literary criticism and form criticism (see below, notes 2 and 3). It takes advantage of the results of these disciplines to identify the units of material and sources available to the evangelists. Literary criticism and form cticism are analytical in their approach to the biblical material, and their ultimate concern is with the individual components of the gospels. Redaction criticism, on the other hand, is synthetic. It seeks to understand the finished product, the entire gospel. It is, therefore, the necessary, final stage in biblical criticism.

For a complete explanation of redaction criticism see:

Perrin, Norman. *What Is Redaction Criticism?* Philadelphia: Fortress, 1969.

Collins, R.F. *Introduction to the New Testament.* New York: Doubleday, 1983, pp. 221-230.

The following are important pioneering works in redaction criticism:

Bornkamm, Günther, Gerhard Barth, and H.J. Held. *Tradition and Interpretation in Matthew.* Philadelphia: Westminster, 1963.

Conzelmann, Hans. *The Theology of Luke.* trans. G. Buswell. New York: Harper & Row, 1960.

Marxsen, Willi. *Mark the Evangelist: Studies in the Redaction History of the Gospel.* Nashville: Abingdon, 1969.

Brown, Raymond E. *The Community of the Beloved Disciple.* New York: Paulist Press, 1979.

Martyn, J. Louis. *History and Theology in the Fourth Gospel.* rev. ed. Nashville: Abingdon, 1979.

2. Form Criticism

Form criticism is a discipline of biblical study that concentrates on the individual units of material in the scriptures. In the gospels these separate segments are called *pericopes*. The purpose of this approach to the Bible is to get behind the sources used by the writers and describe what was happening in the oral tradition. Form criticism is a method of study that investigates the individual units of material and classifies them by form, or *genre;* for example, saying of Jesus, wisdom saying, parable, allegory, miracle story, etc.

These separate units of material circulated in the church in oral form before the gospels were composed. The early church used the pericopes to meet its need to teach and to worship. Each unit, therefore, has a *sitz im leben* ("setting in life"), a situation in the life of the early Christian community, as well as a situation in the life of Jesus, to which it is related. In order to understand the pericope, it is necessary to recognize both its form and its setting in life.

For a complete explanation of form criticism see:

McKnight, Edgar V. *What Is Form Critisicm?* Philadelphia: Fortress, 1969.

The following are classic works about form criticism and the gospels:

> Bultmann, R. *History of the Synoptic Tradition.* trans. J. Marsh. New York: Harper & Row, 1968.
> Dibelius, M. *From Tradition to Gospel.* trans. B.L. Woolf. New York: Scribner, 1934.
> Taylor, V. *The Formation of the Gospel Tradition.* 2nd ed. London: Macmillan, 1935.

3. Literary Criticism

Originally literary criticism was concerned with the authorship of New Testament books and the identification of the literary sources used by the author. A more appropriate term for this discipline would be source criticism.

In the area of gospel study the most important result of this approach has been the demonstration of the interrelatedness of the first three gospels. Literary critics have shown that Mark and the sayings source called Q (see Chapter 3, Note 2) are the major sources used by Matthew and Luke. Research on the Fourth Gospel has produced some evidence that John may have used a signs source.

More recently, literary criticism has lived up to its name by trying to understand the biblical writings as literature. Scholars who take this approach are interested in the relationship between form and content. They emphasize the importance of the imaginative participation of the reader and the function of the story. In fact, they see the gospels as stories that bring the remembered past into the present and enable the reader to take part in the story.

For a complete explanation of literary criticism see:

> Beardslee, William A. *Literary Criticism of the New Testament.* Philadelphia: Fortress, 1970.
> Petersen, N.R. *Literary Criticism for New Testament Critics.* Philadelphia: Fortress, 1978.

The classic work on literary criticism in the original sense and the gospels is:

Streeter, B.H. *The Four Gospels: A Study of Origins.* rev. ed. London: Macmillan, 1930.

A more recent study of the source used by John's gospel is:

Fortna, R.T. *The Gospel of Signs: A Reconstruction of the Narrative Source Underlying the Fourth Gospel.* New York: Cambridge University Press, 1970.

4. Suggested Parallel Versions of the Gospels:

Sparks, H.F.D. *A Synopsis of the Gospels: The Synoptic Gospels with the Johannine Parallels.* Philadelphia: Fortress, 1964.

Throckmorton, B., Jr., ed. *Gospel Parallels: A Synopsis of the First Three Gospels.* 4th ed. Nashville: Nelson, 1979.

Chapter 1

1. The Virgin Birth

The birth of Jesus was not considered extraordinary. When the creeds speak of Jesus being "born of the Virgin Mary" the emphasis is on the word "born." They are affirming Jesus' humanity and his historicity with references to his birth and his death. The credal phrase simply echoes the Pauline formula "born of a woman, born under the Law" (Galatians 4:4). Jesus was born like any child.

It was the conception of Jesus which some early Christians believed to be wonderful. This belief in the virginal conception was not shared by all in the early church. It is not mentioned by Paul, Mark, or John. The only specific references to this tradition are in the birth narratives of Matthew (1:18-25) and Luke (1:26-38).

The biblical evidence leaves the question of the historicity of the virginal conception unresolved. It was part of the tradition before Matthew and Luke composed their gospels. They would not have asked the same questions about its authenticity as modern historians. Undoubtedly they regarded the virginal conception as historical but they told the story for its theological message.

For further details about this tradition see R. Brown's *The Birth of the Messiah,* pages 517-533, which includes a full bibliography on the topic. Brown himself wrote an earlier book on the subject: *The Virginal Conception and the Bodily Resurrection of Jesus* (New York: Paulist, 1973).

2. The Formula Citations

For the formula citations in Matthew see the following:

1:22-23, citing Isaiah 7:14
2:5b-6, citing Micah 5:2 and 2 Samuel 5:2

2:15b, citing Hosea 11:1
2:17-18, citing Jeremiah 31:15
2:23b, citing perhaps Isaiah 4:3 and Judges 16:17
3:3, citing Isaiah 40:3
4:14-16, citing Isaiah 9:1-2
8:17, citing Isaiah 53:4
12:17-21, citing Isaiah 42:1-4
13:14-15, citing Isaiah 6:9-10
13:35, citing Psalm 78:2
21:4-5, citing Isaiah 62:11 and Zechariah 9:9
26:56, a formula without citation
27:9-10, citing Zechariah 11:12-13 with echoes, perhaps, of Jeremiah (32:6-15, 18:2-3)

For the formula citations in the other gospels see the following:

Mark 15:28, citing Isaiah 53:12
Luke 18:31, a formula without citation
Luke 22:37, citing Isaiah 53:12
Luke 24:44, a formula without citation

In John the usage is not as standardized as it is in Matthew, although there are nine fulfillment formulas in the Fourth Gospel. Five times John refers vaguely to the fulfillment of "the scriptures." Only once does he refer to the fulfillment of "the prophet" (12:38, citing Isaiah 53:1). In two instances fulfillment refers to previous words of Jesus (18:9, 32). John's citations from the Old Testament are not always easily identifiable.

For further details, see R. Brown's *The Birth of the Messiah,* page 97, note 2.

3. Similarity Between Luke 1-2 and Acts

There is a strong similarity between the material in Luke 1-2 and Acts. There are features in these first two chapters which are characteristic of Acts but which do not predominate in the rest of Luke's gospel.

One is the references to the outpouring of the Spirit. Compare Luke 1:15, 41, 67, 80, and 2:25, 27 with Acts 2:17. Another is the angelic appearances. Compare Luke 1:11, 26, and 2:9 with Acts 5:19, 8:26, 10:3, 12:7, and 27:23. A third is the use of the title "Christ the Lord." Compare Luke 2:11 with the speeches in Acts, for example, Acts 2:36.

For a complete discussion of the relationship of Luke 1-2 to the rest of the gospel and to Acts see R. Brown's *The Birth of the Messiah,* pages 239-250. His conclusion is that Luke 1-2 were a prologue to Luke's gospel, which the evangelist added when he completed Acts. It forms the introduction to the finished work of Luke-Acts.

4. The Personification of Wisdom

The chief sources for the personification of Wisdom are Job 28, Proverbs 1-9, Baruch 3:9-4:4, Sirach 1,4:11-19, 6:18-31, 14:20-15:10,24 and Wisdom 6-9. Divine Wisdom is a female figure since the Hebrew word for wisdom, *hokmah,* is feminine.

Wisdom is described as existing with God from the beginning, even before the creation of earth (see Proverbs 8:22-23, Sirach 24:9, Wisdom 6:22). Wisdom is portrayed as an emanation of the glory of God (see Wisdom 7:25) and the everlasting light of God (Wisdom 7:26; see also Wisdom 7:10,29). Wisdom descends from heaven to dwell with human beings (Proverbs 8:31, Sirach 24:8, Baruch 3:37, Wisdom 9:10).

The function of Wisdom is to teach people the things that are above (Job 11:6-7, Wisdom 9:16-18), to utter the truth (Proverbs 8:7, Wisdom 6:22), and to give instructions as to what pleases God and how to do God's will (Wisdom 8:4, 9:9-10) in order to lead the people to life (Proverbs 4:13, 8:31-35, Sirach 4:12, Baruch 4:1) and immortality (Wisdom 6:18-19).

The parallels between this description of divine Wisdom and the prologue to the Fourth Gospel, indeed to the main themes of the entire gospel, are obvious. In John's gospel Jesus is the Word who was in the beginning (1:1) with the Father before the world existed (17:5). Jesus manifests the Father's glory to humankind (1:14, 8:50, 11:4, 17:5, 22, 24), and he is the light of the world (1:4-5, 8:12, 9:5). Jesus, too, descends from heaven to dwell among us (1:14, 3:31, 6:38, 16:28), and Jesus' function as revealer is precisely that of Wisdom, according to the Fourth Gospel.

For a detailed discussion of the Wisdom motifs in John's gospel see R. Brown's *The Gospel According to John I-XII,* pages cxxii to cxxv.

5. Recommended Reading

The Birth Stories in Matthew and Luke:
Brown, Raymond E. *The Birth of the Messiah.* Garden City, N.Y.: Doubleday, 1977.

The Prologue to John's Gospel:
Brown, Raymond E. *The Gospel According to John I-XII.* Garden City, N.Y.: Doubleday, 1966, pp. 3-37.

The Inaugural Story in Mark:
Marxen, Willi. *Mark the Evangelist: Studies in the Redaction History of the Gospel.* Nashville: Abingdon, 1969, pp. 30-53.

Questions for Discussion and Reflection

1. Why is it important to know about the community for which each gospel was composed? What have you discovered so far about these communities?

2. What new perspectives on Jesus have emerged from the comparison of the four Christmas stories?

3. Are the Christmas stories primarily theological or historical?

4. What are the significant differences between the four Christmas stories?

5. What do these Christmas stories have in common?

Chapter 2

1. Mark 13 and the Parallel Passages in Matthew and Luke

Mark 13, the "Marcan Apocalypse," is the evangelist's composition of material from two sources: the Jewish apocalyptic tradition (verses 7, 8, 12, 13b, 14-22, 24-27) plus traditional Christian apocalyptic material (verses 5-6, 9-11, 13a, 23, 28-37). The composition is introduced by verse 3 and prefaced by the saying in verse 2 with its geographical and temporal setting in verse 1.

Note that verses 2-3 look toward the *imminent* destruction of the temple. Verses 5-13 reflect experiences and circumstances in A.D. 66 to 70. Yet, as verses 7 and 10 make clear, the End *(eschaton)* has not come. Verse 13 is a reference to martyrs. So verses 5-13 mark the beginning of the End.

The reference to "the desolating sacrilege" in verse 14 provides us with an important clue. For Mark the desolating sacrilege is not the altar to Zeus erected in the temple by Antiochus Epiphanes in 167 B.C. (see Daniel 11:31, also 9:27, 12:11, and 1 Maccabees 1:54). It is so identified in the parallel passage, in Matthew (24:15) but Mark makes no specific reference to Daniel. Mark's readers will understand that the desolating sacrilege is "Caesar's Image," the statue of Caligula which he directed P. Petronius, the procurator, to erect in the temple in A.D. 40. The emperor's death the next year prevented this order from being carried out, but the threat of desecration was obviously in the minds of Jews and early Christians alike.

The second half of Mark 13:14 presupposes that the seige of Jerusalem is imminent. It will be experienced by "this generation" (verse 30), that is, the congregation for whom Mark composed his gospel. The exact time of the End, however, is known only to the Father (verse 32). So Mark exhorts his congregation to watch (verses 33-37), to be alert and wait expectantly for the Second Coming of the risen Christ (the *Parousia*).

The Marcan Apocalypse undergoes some significant changes in Luke's version (Luke 21:5-36). Luke shifts the emphasis to the future, the epoch of the mission of the church to the nations (see Luke 21:24-25). He omits Mark 13:10. Luke exhorts his readers who are engaged in the mission to resist temptation (21:8) because for him the End is far removed.

Luke's reference to the seige of Jerusalem in 21:20 is an important clue because his description of Jerusalem surrounded by armies is very explicit and accurate. It could only have been written after the fall of the city in A.D. 70. Notice that for Luke this is the predicted desolation. So Luke 21:8-24 was composed after A.D. 70.

Luke omits Mark 13:21-23 with the warning of the appearance of false messiahs and assures his readers, instead, that the church will be preserved in time of persecution. Note how Luke changes the reference to "this generation"—which for Mark meant his own generation—to a reference to the Jews in the epoch before the ministry of Jesus (21:32). So Luke turned the apocalyptic prediction of Mark 13 into utterances of the historical Jesus, and he brought this prophecy up to date after the events of A.D. 70.

Matthew's parallel to Mark 13 (chapter 24) is part of a speech complex (Matthew 23-25) which contains topically related material. For Matthew the *Parousia* is still to come, and he leaves the date completely open (see 24:3). The sign, the desolating sacrilege, is no longer a reference to the events in A.D. 40 but, according to Matthew (24:15), it is the classic symbol from Daniel. The emphasis in the chapter is on the developing mission of the church and not, as in Mark, on the imminent Second Coming of the risen Christ. Matthew also inserts his chapter 25 between this passage and his passion narrative. (See the discussion of Matthew's Good Friday story in Chapter 3 for the significance of this.)

Mark 13, then, is all one sermon, a single exhortation by the risen Lord himself to his followers in Galilee to be on the alert for his imminent *Parousia*.

Matthew 24 is part of a collection of sermons in which the risen Lord proclaims during the missionary period of the church what, for Matthew, is identical to what the historical Jesus said.

In Luke 21 the historical Jesus is the speaker, and he is speaking about the end of the epoch of Israel.

2. The Evangelists' Use of Geography

Geography is primarily of theological significance in the gospels. Obviously the evangelists base their geographic setting for the gospel on what is known to the tradition in broad terms of the historical ministry of Jesus. Jesus grew up in Nazareth. One part of the tradition said he was born in Bethlehem. His public ministry was in Galilee, largely centered in the region around the Sea of Galilee. He was crucified and buried just outside the city of Jerusalem. Each gospel writer, however, used this general geographical setting in his own way to enhance his particular proclamation of the gospel, that is, for his theological purpose.

Mark composed a Galilean gospel. According to this evangelist, Jesus came from Nazareth and was at home in Capernaum. Except for a visit by Jesus to Tyre and Sidon (7:24-31) and the identification of him as Messiah by his disciples at Caesarea Philippi (8:27-30), the entire public ministry of Jesus is set in Galilee and the region around the Sea of Galilee. People came from all over to Galilee to see Jesus (3:7-8). He never goes to Jerusalem until he journeys there, through Perea—"beyond the Jordan" (10:1)—which was attached to Galilee, for the final week of his ministry which culminated in his crucifixion.

So Mark has imposed a geographical scheme upon his version of the gospel story. The first half of his gospel is set in Galilee (chapters 1-9). Then, after a transitional chapter (10), the other half of his gospel is set in Jerusalem (chapters 11-16). Finally, in his version of the Easter story Mark emphasizes the command to the disciples to go back to Galilee, there to await the return of the risen Lord (16:7).

To some extent the other Synoptic gospels, Matthew and Luke, follow this Marcan scheme. But each of these evangelists modifies and adapts Mark's geographical structure to suit his own purpose. For Matthew, Galilee represents the territory of the Gentiles (4:15) and Jesus' ministry there fulfills the prophecy in Isaiah 9:1-2. In his story of the empty tomb, Matthew places the emphasis on the announcement that Christ is risen, not on the command to return to Galilee. He does place the commissioning of the Eleven in Galilee, but this is most likely because he wants to set this final incident in his gospel on the mountain (28:16), the same setting he uses for Jesus' proclamation of the new Torah (5:1).

Luke is less interested in Galilee as a place than in the Galileans who are the "witnesses" who go up to Jerusalem with Jesus. Judea and, in particular, Jerusalem are the important places in this gospel. Luke omits Mark 6:45-8:27 from his gospel and he does not refer to Samaria and Perea in Luke 3:1. So in this gospel Jesus does not travel to Phoenicia, the Decapolis, or Perea.

Moreover, Luke's knowledge of the region is not precise. He appears to view the country much as a pious Christian who has never been to Israel visualizes the Holy Land. In one place he describes Jesus going to Jerusalem by "passing along between Samaria and Galilee" (17:11). In another passage he locates Galilee directly adjacent to Judea (4:44, 5:17). According to Luke, when Jesus makes his journey to Jerusalem he goes through Samaria to Jericho (see 17:11 and 18:35), a curious combination of the two different routes from Galilee to Jerusalem. Even Luke's knowledge of Jerusalem, which is such an important place in his gospel, is sketchy. Anyone reading just this gospel would assume that everything in Jerusalem took place on the Mount of Olives or in the temple.

This is not the case in John's gospel. The Fourth Evangelist provides even the modern pilgrim with a reasonable guide to Jerusalem. John also departs from Mark's geographical scheme and records several journeys of Jesus to Jerusalem and Judea (2:13, 3:22, 4:3, 7:10, 10:22-23, 11:7). With the exception of the references to the presentation of Jesus in the temple and the visit of the twelve-year-old Jesus to the temple in the prologue to Luke's gospel (2:22-52), in the Synoptic gospels Jesus journeys once, only, to Jerusalem. Obviously John's account of several journeys of Jesus to Jerusalem is more accurate historically.

John also describes a visit by Jesus to Samaria and a mission to the Samaritans (chapter 4). There is no mention of this in the Synoptic gospels. Luke, at least, seems to reserve all mention of a ministry to Samaria for the early mission of the church described in Acts.

It is quite clear that geography is of theological, not historical, significance in the gospels. For further details of the theological significance of geography in the gospels consult the following:

> Marxsen, Willi. *Mark the Evangelist: Studies in the Redaction History of the Gospels,* Nashville: Abingdon, 1969, pp. 54-116.
>
> Conzelmann, Hans. *The Theology of Luke.* New York: Harper & Row, 1960, pp. 18-136.
>
> Fortna, R.T. "Theological Use of Locale in the Fourth Gospel," *Anglican Theological Review,* sup. series 3 (1974) pp. 58-75.

3. Jewish Guards at the Tomb

The legend of the stealing of Jesus' body by his disciples was part of the tradition. It is reported more fully in the apocryphal Gospel of Peter 8:29-11:49 and 12:50-13:57.

4. The Element of Doubt in the Resurrection Tradition

There is an element of doubt that appears to be part of the resurrection tradition. Matthew makes a passing reference to some of the Eleven who doubted (28:17) when they were confronted by the risen Christ before their commissioning. Luke reports that the Eleven dismissed the news of the women who found the tomb empty as an idle tale (24:11). Luke also portrays Cleopas and his friend as expressing their doubts to the stranger who walks with them back to Emmaus (24:13-27; see also 24:41).

It is John, however, who emphasizes this theme of doubting. He devotes an entire episode in his Easter story to the appearance of the risen Christ to the disciple who has ever since been known as "doubting Thomas" (20:24-29). John is particularly concerned to strengthen the faith of those who did not see and yet believed, those members of the community of the Beloved Disciple.

This detail, this element of doubt, seems to have crept into the Easter tradition after the time of Paul and Mark.

5. Recommended Reading for Further Information About the Easter Stories

Brown, Raymond E. *The Gospel According to John XXIII-XXI*. Garden City, N.Y.: Doubleday, 1970, pp. 965-1132.

Fuller, R.H. *The Formation of the Resurrection Narratives*. rev. ed. New York: Macmillan, 1980.

Perrin, Norman. *The Resurrection According to Matthew, Mark and Luke*. Philadelphia: Fortress, 1977.

Questions for Discussion and Reflection

1. Why is the Easter story the key to the proclamation of good news by the evangelists?

2. Are the Easter stories primarily historical or theological?

3. What is the distinctive emphasis of each of the four Easter stories?

4. What important clues to the purpose of each gospel do these four Easter stories give us?

5. Is the purpose revealed by the Easter story in each gospel reflected in that gospel's Christmas story?

Chapter 3

1. The Title "Son of Man" in the Gospels

The title "Son of man" appears in all the gospels. In the Synoptics it is the title Jesus uses most frequently, and in these three gospels only Jesus uses this title.

The Son of man is a late Jewish apocalyptic figure who is to come on the clouds of heaven and preside over the events leading to the end of the world. He will rule over all in the everlasting kingdom, and he will judge the world. The hope for such a heaven-sent Messiah is based on a development of the vision in Daniel 7:13-14.

The title "Son of man," however, is used in three different ways in the gospels. First, it is used as an emphatic way of saying "man" or "I." It is used to identify the earthly activity of Jesus who has authority to forgive sins (Mark 2:10-12), who is lord of the sabbath (Mark 2:27-28), who is a glutton and a drunkard, a friend of tax collectors and sinners (Matthew 11:19), and who has nowhere to lay his head (Matthew 8:20). There is no messianic implication in this use of the title.

Second, the title "Son of man" is applied to Jesus to describe him as the present, suffering Messiah (see, for example, Mark 8:31, 9:31, 10:33-34, 10:45). The predictions of the passion in these sayings are too accurate to have been spoken before the crucifixion and resurrection. In these passages the title of Son of man was attributed to Jesus by the early church. It was part of the process, along with identifying Jesus with the suffering servant of the Old Testament, of explaining the necessity for his death.

Third, and most important, there are a significant number of passages in which the title refers to the apocalyptic figure who is to come, a future, glorious Son of man. Mark 8:38 is a good example of the sayings in this category: "For whoever is ashamed of me and of my words in this adulterous and sinful generation, of him will the Son of man also be ashamed, when he comes in the glory of his Father with the holy angels." The saying in the Marcan Apocalypse (13:26-27) — "And then they will see the Son of man coming in clouds with great power and glory. And then he will send out the angels, and gather his elect from the four winds, from the ends of the earth to the ends of heaven" — is echoed by Jesus' reply to the High Priest at his trial before the Sanhedrin (Mark 14:62). For other apocalyptic Son of man sayings see Luke 12:40, 17:22-30, 18:8, 21:36, Matthew 13:41-43, 19:28, 24:26-44, 25:31-33, John 1:51, 3:13, 5:26-29, 6:62.

In these sayings Jesus usually refers to someone other than himself, a Son of man who is still to come. A good example of such a reference is the saying in Luke 12:8-9: "And I tell you, everyone who acknowledges me before men, the Son of man also will acknowledge before the angels of God; but he who denies me before men will be denied before the angels of God." The saying in Mark 8:38, quoted above, with the parallel in Luke 9:26, is another example. Further examples are found in Matthew 24:44 (Luke 12:40), Luke 17:22-30 (Matthew 24:26-28, 37-39), and Luke 11:30 (Matthew 12:40).

The Son of man sayings in this category are the most numerous, and they are found throughout the gospels — in Mark, Q, the special material in Matthew and Luke, and in John. They are probably authentic sayings of Jesus. In the context of the Jewish apocalyptic hope so characteristic of his day, Jesus was pointing ahead to the coming of the glorious Son of man. After the resurrection the church identified Jesus himself with this apocalyptic Son of man.

2. Q — The Sayings Source

Scholars discovered the sayings source they call Q by a simple comparison of the material in the Synoptic gospels. Their study led, first, to the discovery that Matthew and Luke included most of Mark's gospel in their versions. Six hundred verses, or 57 percent of Matthew, came from Mark, and 504 verses, or 43 percent of Luke, came from Mark. Second, they found some material unique to Matthew (200 verses or 27 percent of Matthew) and some material that occurs only in Luke (500 verses or 43 percent of Luke). Finally, they discovered 170 verses (16 percent of Matthew and 14 percent of Luke) that were in both Matthew and Luke, *but not in Mark!* The hypothesis based on this discovery is that these 170 verses form a second written source used by Matthew and Luke. For convenience the scholars named this source Q—the first letter of the German word for "source."

Q contains the earliest written material concerning Jesus. It appears to be a collection of sayings arranged in a topical, and not a chronological, order. There is only one miracle story in Q, and there is no reference to the passion nor any mention of the resurrection.

The material is primarily eschatological in tone. It contains eschatological warnings. All the citations of the Q material that follow are Luke's: 3:7-9, 16b-17; 6:37-42; 10:13-15, 11:39-52; 12:49-53, 54-56, 57-59; 13:24-29, 34-35; 17:23-37. There are references to eschatological conflict: 4:1-12; 11:14-22; 24-26; and to eschatological promise: 6:20-23, 27-36; 11:1-4, 9-13; 22:29-30. Some of the sayings reflect an interest in eschatological knowledge: 10:21-24; and eschatological discipleship: 9:57-58; 10:1-12; 12:2-12; 14:25-27. There are some eschatological parables: 12:39-40, 42-46; 13:20-21; 14:16-24; 15:4-7. The material from this source portrays Jesus as the eschatological messenger and bringer of salavation: 7:19-23, 24-35; 11:29b-32.

This source came from a Christian community in the middle of the first century. It was a community that expected the final judgment and the eschatological vindication to be imminent. For this community Jesus was the martyred, eschatological prophet soon to be vindicated by God.

The theory of the existence of such a sayings source was supported by the discovery in 1945 of the Gospel of Thomas (see note 6, Chapter 4). This document is *not* the same as Q, but it is a document of a similar type, a collection of sayings of Jesus. The hypothesis that Matthew and Luke used a written source which contained sayings of Jesus is all the more plausible now that a similar first-century collection of Jesus' sayings has been discovered.

For further information about Q see: Howard C. Kee, *Jesus in History,* second edition, New York: Harcourt Brace Jovanovich, 1977, pp. 76-120. Pages 85-87 provide a list of all the Q material.

3. The Role of Pilate in the Trial of Jesus

In Mark (15:6-15), Pilate attempts to have Jesus released, but he has no reluctance to sentence him.

In Matthew (27:19, 24-25), Pilate's wife warns him to have nothing to do with Jesus, who she learned from a dream was righteous. Pilate, after unsuccessfully trying to release Jesus, washes his hands of the whole matter.

In Luke, Pilate finds Jesus innocent three times (23:4, 14, 22). He sends him to Herod Antipas in an effort to avoid sentencing him (23:6-16). When that fails he offers a compromise to the Jewish authorities, which they reject (23:16, 23).

In John, Pilate makes a determined effort to pardon Jesus. He insists the Jews try Jesus by their own law (18:31). He finds Jesus innocent and offers to release him (18:39). Again he brings Jesus before the crowd to proclaim his innocence (19:4), and when the chief priests and officers cry out for his crucifixion, Pilate says once more, "Take him yourselves and crucify him, for I find no crime in him" (19:6). Then he pleads with Jesus to defend himself so that he will have grounds to release him (19:10). Finally, Pilate does attempt to release Jesus (19:12), but he is prevented by the accusation of the Jews that if he pardons Jesus he is not Caesar's friend. Once more, at the moment of passing sentence, Pilate tries to free Jesus. "Shall I crucify your king?" he asks. But the chief priests answer, "We have no king but Caesar." At this, Pilate hands Jesus over to them to be crucified (19:15-16).

The pattern is obvious. In Mark, the earliest account of

the trial, Pilate shares the responsibility for ordering the crucifixion of Jesus. In successive accounts he assumes, more and more, the role of an official who wants to release Jesus but is prevented from doing so by the Jews. In John, the latest account, the Jews force Pilate to act against his better judgment by bringing political pressure to bear against him. Later Christians made it clear that the Jews, not the Romans, were responsible for Jesus' death. But note, in contrast, that Mark in his passion narrative stresses the point that Jesus went to his death willingly. According to this gospel, nobody took Jesus' life. He gave it!

4. Evidence for the Site of Jesus' Trial

Modern pilgrims follow the Via Dolorosa, the traditional way of the cross, from the site of the Antonia in the northwest corner of the temple area to the Church of the Holy Sepulchre, the site of Golgotha and the tomb. This route was marked out when the Antonia, a fortress built by Herod the Great, was considered the official residence, the "praetorium," of the Roman prefects when they were in Jerusalem.

All the evidence, however, points to the larger palace built by Herod the Great, the "upper palace" or Citadel by the Jaffa Gate in the upper city. This was where Pilate stayed when he was in Jerusalem, and this is where the trial took place. The Antonia was the barracks for the Roman troops.

For the archaeological and historical evidence supporting this site for the trial of Jesus see the following:

> Murphy-O'Connor, Jerome. *The Holy Land*. Oxford: Oxford University Press, 1980, pp. 19-20.
>
> Wilkinson, John. *Jerusalem as Jesus Knew It*. London: Thames and Hudson, 1978, pp. 137-142.

5. Recommended Reading on the Good Friday Stories:

> Brown, R.E. *A Crucified Christ in Holy Week*. Collegeville: Liturgical Press, 1986.

Donahue, J.R. *Are You the Christ? The Trial Narrative in the Gospel of Mark.* Missoula, Montana: Society of Biblical Literature, 1973.

Evans, C.F. *Explorations in Theology 2.* London: SCM, 1977, pp. 3-66.

Senior, D.P. *The Passion Narrative According to Matthew.* Leuven: University Press, 1975.

Sloyan, G.S. *Jesus on Trial: The Development of the Passion Narratives and Their Historical and Ecumenical Implications.* Philadelphia: Fortress, 1973.

Questions for Discussion and Reflection

1. What does the relatively fixed form of the passion narrative tell us about the significance of Jesus' death for the early church?

2. How were the evangelists able to adapt the passion story to suit their purposes?

3. In the long run, are the historical discrepancies in the four versions of the passion narrative important?

4. Does the passion narrative in each gospel reflect the purpose revealed by the Easter story in that gospel?

5. What does each evangelist's passion story tell you about the community for which he composed his gospel?

Chapter 4

1. Tools of the Trade

For serious Bible study you will need the following tools of the trade:

A. Study Bible Contemporary versions provide the best translations of the most up-to-date text of the original, and a fresh translation of a familiar passage will often pique your interest. You will find a critical edition of the Bible with introductions to each book and explanatory notes on the text very useful for study. Recommended study Bible:

> May, Herbert G. and Bruce M. Metzger, eds. *The New Oxford Annotated Bible with the Apocrypha: Expanded Edition*. Revised Standard Version. New York: Oxford University Press, 1973.

B. Commentary Next to the text itself, the most important tool for the study of the Bible is a commentary. Libraries, including parish libraries, often have at least a one-volume commentary on the Bible, and there are inexpensive commentaries on each of the gospels in the Pelican series. These are quite satisfactory, and Dennis Nineham's commentary on Mark is excellent.

A good commentary is an indispensable help to the study of the gospels. Like an experienced and knowledgeable guide, it will provide you with important background information, and it will take you through the gospel, pointing out significant passages you might miss and supplying an explanation of verses you might otherwise misunderstand. Recommended commentaries:

> Brown, R.E. *The Gospel According to John*. 2 vols. Garden City, N.Y.: Doubleday, 1966, 1970 (Anchor Bible).

Caird, G.B. *The Gospel of St. Luke.* Baltimore: Penguin, 1963.

Danker, F. *Jesus and the New Age according to Luke.* St. Louis: Clayton, 1983.

Fenton, J.C. *The Gospel of St. Matthew.* Baltimore: Penguin, 1963.

Fitzmyer, J. *The Gospel according to Luke.* 2 vols. Garden City, N.Y.: Doubleday, 1985, 1986 (Anchor Bible).

Gundry, P.H. *Matthew, A Commentary on His Literary and Theological Art.* Grand Rapids: Eerdmans, 1982.

Kysar, R. *The Augsburg Commentary on the New Testament: John.* Minneapolis: Augsburg, 1986.

Marsh, J. *The Gospel of St. John.* Baltimore: Penguin, 1968.

Nineham, D.E. *The Gospel of St. Mark.* Baltimore: Penguin, 1963.

Schnackenburg, R. *The Gospel according to St. John.* 3 vols. New York: Crossroad, 1980, 1982.

Schweizer, E. *The Good News according to Luke.* Trans. D.E. Green. Atlanta: John Knox, 1984.

———. *The Good News according to Mark.* Trans. D.H. Madvig. Atlanta: John Knox, 1970.

———. *The Good News according to Matthew.* Trans. D.E. Green. Atlanta: John, Knox, 1975.

Taylor, V. *The Gospel according to St. Mark.* 2nd ed. London: Macmillan, 1966.

You will also find that the following tools are useful on certain occasions:

C. Concordance If you want to locate a certain passage, or find all the passages where a certain word is used, you will find a concordance useful. In a concordance, citations of biblical passages are listed under the principal words found in the Bible. For example, if you want to know where in Mark to find the phrase "take up his cross and follow me," you can look up "cross" (or "follow") and go down the list of citations until you find the reference you want. If you want to know where the word "faith" is used in the Bible, you can simply look it up and find all the references listed book by book. Analytical concordances, which separate the citations for each English word into the various Hebrew and Greek words translated by that English word, are particularly helpful. You do not have to know Hebrew or Greek to use them, and yet they put you in touch with the original languages of the Bible. Recommended concordances:

>Morrison, C. *An Analytical Concordance to the Revised Standard Version of the New Testament.* Philadelphia: Westminster, 1979.
>
>Strong, J. *Strong's Exhaustive Concordance of the Bible.* Nashville: Abingdon, 1980 (King James Version).
>
>Young, R. *Young's Analytical Concordance to the Bible.* revised and corrected. Nashville: Nelson, 1982.

D. Bible Dictionary and Theological Word Book A dictionary of the Bible and a theological word book are useful for looking up key terms, significant topics, and important names. Recommended:

>Achtemeier, P., ed. *Harper's Bible Dictionary.* San Francisco: Harper & Row, 1985.
>
>Buttrick, G.A., ed. *The Interpreter's Dictionary of the Bible.* 4 vols. plus supplementary vol. Nashville: Abingdon, 1962.
>
>Richardson, A. *A Theological Word Book of the Bible.* London: SCM, 1950.

E. Bible Atlas You will find an atlas of the Bible helpful for locating sites and getting the lay of the land in the biblical period you are studying. Recommended:

>Groellenberg, L. *Atlas of the Bible.* trans. and ed. by J.M.H. Reid and H.H. Rowley. London: Nelson 1956.

Wright, G.E. and F.V. Filson, eds. *The Westminister Historical Atlas to the Bible.* rev. ed. Philadelphia: Westminster, 1956.

2. See note 2, Chapter 3, for information about Q.

3. See note 1, Chapter 2, for commentary on Mark 13.

4. Exercise One—A Study of the Miracles

This exercise is designed to give you an opportunity to learn more about the miracle stories in Mark and the way he used them. It can then be expanded to include an examination of all the miracle stories in the gospels.

Miracles present a problem for most modern students of the Bible. We have been taught to think in a scientific mode. When we confront a phenomenon the questions that come to our minds are: How did it happen? What caused it? Those who lived in the Biblical period thought in a prephilosophical, prescientific mode. Often they expressed their thoughts in story form. For them miracles posed no problems. They never asked how they happened or what caused them. They had no notion that a miracle interrupted the so-called laws of nature. For them miracles were wonderful. They were signs that evoked awe and pointed to the presence of God in their world.

So the miracle stories in the Bible never give us enough information to satisfy our scientific curiosity. But it is not necessary to explain them, or explain them away. It is better to accept them in the mode in which they were intended to be understood. For those who lived in New Testament times, miracles were wonderful signs of God's activity among us. They may not be as convincing to us as they were to them, but they need not be obstacles to our faith.

You will need a commentary to do this exercise. Pay attention to the differences between the accounts of the miracle story in the various gospels. Note any omissions or additions, and look carefully at the way each evangelist introduces and concludes the story. This exercise will help sharpen your skill in employing the techniques of isolating and comparing the material in one gospel with the parallel passages in the other gospels and identifying the context in which the evangelist placed the material.

Examine the following miracle stories and where possible compare them with their parallels:

Miracle Stories in Mark:
1:23-27; para. Luke 4:33-37
1:29-31; para. Matthew 8:14-17, Luke 4:38-41
1:40-45; para. Matthew 8:2-4, Luke 5:12-16
2:1-12; para. Matthew 9:1-8, Luke 5:17-26
3:1-6; para. Matthew 12:9-14, Luke 6:6-11
4:35-41; para.. Matthew 8:18,23-27, Luke 8:22-25
5:1-20; para. Matthew 8:28-34, Luke 8:26-39
5:22-43; para. Matthew 9:18-26, Luke 8:40-56
6:30-44; para. Matthew 14:13-21, Luke 9:10-17, John
    6:1-13 and Mark 8:1-10; para. Matthew 15:32-39
6:45-52; para. Matthew 14:22-33 (cf. John 6:15-21)
7:24-30; para. Matthew 15:21-28
7:31-37; para. Matthew 15:29-31 (cf. Matthew 9:32-34)
9:14-29; para. Matthew 17:14-21, Luke 9:37-42
10:46-52; para. Matthew 20:29-34, Luke 18:35-43 (see
    Mark 8:22-26, Matthew 9:27-31, John 9:1-7)
11:12-14,20-25; para. Matthew 21:18-22

Miracle Story in Q:
Matthew 8:5-13; para. Luke 7:1-10 (see John 4:46-53)

Miracle Stories found only in Luke:
Luke 5:1-11 (see John 21:1-4), 7:11-17, 13:10-17, 14:1-6, 17:11-19

Signs in John:
2:1-11, 4:46-54, 5:1-9, 6:1-13, 6:15-21, 9:1-7, 11:1-44

Resources for the study of the miracles:

Fuller, R.H. *Interpreting the Miracles.* Philadelphia: Westminster, 1963.

Theissen, G. *Miracle Stories of the Early Christian Tradition.* trans. F. McDonagh. Philadelphia: Fortress, 1983.

5. Exercise Two — A Comparison of the Teachings of Jesus in Matthew and Luke

The second exercise is designed to give you a chance to continue the comparison of selected passages from Matthew's Sermon on the Mount with the parallel passages in Luke. Use a commentary, and pay particular attention to the way each evangelist adapts the material to his own context. Compare:

Matthew 5:38-48 with Luke 6:27-36
Matthew 6:9-13 with Luke 11:2-4
Matthew 6:22-23 with Luke 11:33-36
Matthew 6:25-33 with Luke 12:22-31
Matthew 7:15-20 with Luke 6:43-45
Matthew 7:24-27 with Luke 6:47-49

When you have completed the comparisons it would be a good idea to read Matthew 5-7 straight through to get the impact of his presentation of the new Torah.

If you wish to expand this exercise to include a comparison of all the Q material in Matthew and Luke, you will find a list of the Q material on pages 85-87 of Howard C. Kee's *Jesus in History* (second edition). The citations are to Luke. To find the parallels in Matthew, use the cross references in a critical text of Luke.

Recommended reading on the Sermon on the Mount:

Davis, W.D. *The Setting of the Sermon on the Mount.* Cambridge: Cambridge University Press, 1964.
Guelich, R.A. *The Sermon on the Mount: A Foundation for Understanding.* Waco, Texas: Word, 1982.
Suggs, M.J. *Wisdom, Christology and Law in Matthew's Gospel.* Cambridge, Mass. Harvard University Press, 1970.

6. The Gospel of Thomas

The Gospel of Thomas was discovered in 1945 as part of a library of documents found at Nag Hammadi in Egypt. It has only been recently, however, that these documents have been available in English. For the English translation of these texts see:

> Robinson, James M., ed. *The Nag Hammadi Library in English.* San Francisco: Harper & Row, 1977.

The text of the Gospel of Thomas is on pages 118-130. The editor's introduction gives information about the discovery of the documents.

Recently, one scholar called Thomas "The Fourth Synoptic Gospel" and ranked it alongside the first three gospels as a source of information on the life and teachings of Jesus. It contains a series of 114 sayings attributed to Jesus, without narrative, without a birth story or a passion narrative, and without any accounts of miracles. It is similar to, but independent of, the sayings source Q.

For information about the importance of the Gospel of Thomas see the following:

> Davies, Stevan. "Thomas the Fourth Synoptic Gospel." *Biblical Archaeologist.* vol. 46, no. 1. (Winter, 1983), pp. 6-14.
>
> Davies, Stevan. *The Gospel of Thomas and Christian Wisdom.* Minneapolis: Winston, 1983.
>
> Kee, H.C. *Jesus in History.* second edition. New York: Harcourt Brace, Jovanovich, 1977, pp. 274-280.

7. *The Nag Hammadi Library in English.* p. 128.

8. *The Nag Hammadi Library in English.* p. 125.

9. Exercise Three—A Study of the Parables

A parable is an extension of the wisdom sentence. It is a story, taken from everyday life, told to teach a single lesson.

It differs from an allegory which is a story in which every element has a second, hidden meaning. Compare, for example, the parable of the sower (Mark 4:3-9) with the allegorical interpretation of the parable (Mark 4:13-20). The parable is a story of encouragement. It assures whoever hears it that, despite all the signs to the contrary, the kingdom of God is coming. The allegorical interpretation, on the other hand, is an exhortation to those who await the coming of the kingdom to accept the word and let it bear fruit in their lives. As you investigate the parables, watch for those that have been turned into allegories or given an allegorical interpretation.

The third exercise is designed to let you expand your investigation of the well known parables found only in Luke to include a survey of all the parables found in the gospels. There are six parables in Mark, nine in Q, ten unique to Matthew, fifteen found only in Luke, and three that occur only in John. There are parallels to twelve of the parables in the Gospel of Thomas.

Parables in Mark:
4:3-8; para. Matthew 13:3-8, Luke 8:5-8, Thomas 9
4:26-29
4:30-32; para. Matthew 13:31-32, Luke 13:18-19,
    Thomas 20
12:1-11; para. Matthew 21:33-44, Luke 20:9-18,
    Thomas 65
13:28-29; para. Matthew 24:32-33, Luke 21:29-31
13:33-37; para. Luke 12:35-38

Parables in Q (in Matthew and parallels):
5:25-26; para. Luke 12:58-59
11:16-19; para. Luke 7:31-35
12:43-45; para. Luke 11:24-26
13:33; para. Luke 13:20-21, Thomas 96
18:12-14; para. Luke 15:4-7, Thomas 107
22:1-10; para. Luke 14:16-24, Thomas 64
24:43-44; para. Luke 12:39-40, Thomas 21b, 103
24:45-51; para. Luke 12:42-46

25:14-30; para. Luke 19:12-27

Parables found only in Matthew:
13:24-30; para. Thomas 57
13:44; para. Thomas 109
13:45-46, para. Thomas 76
13:47-48
18:23-35
20:1-16
21:28-32
22:11-14
25:1-13
25:31-46

Parables found only in Luke:
7:41-43
10:25-37
11:5-8
12:16-21; para. Thomas 63
13:6-9
13:25-30
14:7-11
14:28-32
15:8-10
15:11-32
16:1-8
16:19-31
17:7-10
18:1-8
18:9-14

Parables in John:
10:1-6
10:7-18
15:1-6

Parables in Thomas, not in the New Testament:
97
98

The classic resource for studying the parables is:

Jeremias, J. *The Parables of Jesus.* trans. S.H. Hooke. rev. ed. New York: Scribner, 1966. (A simplified version is available under the title *Rediscovering the Parables.)*

Also recommended:

Carlston, C.E. *The Parables of the Triple Tradition.* Phildelphia: Fortress, 1975.

Lambrecht, J. *Once More Astonished: The Parables of Jesus.* rev. ed. New York: Crossroad, 1981.

10. Exercise Four — A Study of the Teaching Units in John

This exercise is planned to give you an opportunity to investigate the rest of the teaching units in John's gospel.

3:1-21, 31-36 — Discourse with Nicodemus
4:7-42 — Discourse with the Samaritan woman
5 — Jesus and the sabbath
7, 8, 9 — Jesus and the feast of Tabernacles
10 — Jesus and the feast of the Dedication
11:1-44 — Raising of Lazarus and discourse on resurrection

Analyze each passage thoroughly. You will have to use a commentary to do this, preferably:

Brown, R.E. *The Gospel According to John I-XII.* Garden City; N.Y.: Doubleday, 1966.

11. Recommended reading for further information about the four gospels:

Kee, H.C. *Jesus in History: An Approach to the Study of the Gospels.* 2nd ed. New York: Harcourt Brace Jovanovitch, 1977.

Rohde, J. *Rediscovering the Teaching of the Evangelists.* trans. D.M. Barton. Philadelphia: Westminster, 1968.

For further bibliography on the four gospels see the list of suggested reading at the end of this book. For a detailed bibliography on Mark and Matthew, see:

Stanton, G., ed. *The Interpretation of Matthew.* Philadelphia: Fortress, 1983, pp. 156-161.

Telford, W., ed. *The Interpretation of Mark.* Philadelphia: Fortress, 1985, pp. 167-174.

Questions for Discussion and Reflection

1. Why is it important to recognize that the gospels are theological documents?
2. Why is it necessary to see each gospel as a whole?
3. What are the basic techniques of the approach to the study of the gospels proposed in this book? How can this approach be applied to a study of the gospels?
4. What is the purpose of using this approach to study the gospels?
5. Why is it important to let all four gospels have their say?

Conclusion

1. Tatian's Diatesseron

For a sample of Tatian's *Diatesseron* see the excerpt in an English translation in H.C. Kee's *Jesus in History,* second edition, pp. 285-289.

2. Contemporary Studies of Jesus

The classic studies of Jesus are:

Bornkamm, Günther. *Jesus of Nazareth.* trans. Irene and Fraser McLuskey with James Robinson. New York: Harper & Row, 1960.

Conzelmann, Hans. *Jesus: The Classic Article from RGG,* expanded and updated. trans. J. Raymond Lord. Philadelphia: Fortress, 1973.

A recent excellent study in a more popular form is:

Sloyan, Gerard S. *Jesus in Focus: A Life in Its Setting.* Mystic, Conn.: Twenty-Third Publications, 1983.

Suggestions for Further Reading

For the General Reader

Edwards, O.C. *Luke's Story of Jesus*. Philadelphia: Fortress, 1981.

Edwards. R.A. *Matthew's Story of Jesus*. Philadelphia: Fortress, 1985.

Kelber, W.H. *Mark's Story of Jesus*. Philadelphia: Fortress, 1979.

Kysar, R. *John's Story of Jesus*. Philadelphia: Fortress, 1984.

Sloyan, G.S. *Jesus in Focus: A Life in Its Setting*. Mystic, Conn.: Twenty-Third Publications, 1983.

For the More Serious Reader and the Student

Mark

Best, E. *Mark: The Gospel as Story*. Edinburgh: T.&T. Clark, 1983.

Kee, H.C. *Community of the New Age: Studies in Mark's Gospel*. Philadelphia: Westminster, 1977.

Kermode, F. *The Genesis of Secrecy. On the Interpretation of Narrative*. Cambridge, Mass.: Harvard University Press, 1979.

Kingsbury, J.D. *The Christology of Mark's Gospel*. Philadelphia: Fortress, 1983.

Rhoads, D. and D. Michie. *Mark as Story: An Introduction to the Narrative of a Gospel*. Philadelphia: Fortress, 1982.

Weeden, T.J. *Mark: Traditions in Conflict*. Philadelphia: Fortress, 1971.

Matthew

Cope, O.L. *Matthew: A Scribe Trained for the Kingdom of Heaven.* Washington, D.C.: Catholic Biblical Association, 1976.

Ellis, P.F. *Matthew: His Mind and His Message.* Collegeville, Minn.: Liturgical Press, 1974.

Kingsbury, J.D. *Matthew: Structure, Christology and Kingdom.* Philadelphia: Fortress, 1975.

Meier, J.P. *The Vision of Matthew: Christ, Church and Morality in the First Gospel.* New York: Paulist Press, 1979.

Minear, P.S. *Matthew: The Teacher's Gospel.* New York: Pilgrim Press, 1982.

Luke

Cassidy, R.J. *Jesus, Politics and Society: A Study of Luke's Gospel.* Maryknoll, N.Y.: Orbis, 1978.

____and P.J. Scharper, eds. *Political Issues in Luke-Acts.* Maryknoll, N.Y.: Orbis, 1983.

Jervell, J. *Luke and the People of God: A New Look at Luke-Acts.* Minneapolis: Augsburg, 1979.

Juel, D. *Luke-Acts: The Promise of History.* Atlanta: John Knox, 1983.

Karris, R.J. *Luke, Artist and Theologian.* Mahwah, N.J.: Paulist Press, 1985.

Pilgrim, W.E. *Good News to the Poor: Wealth and Poverty in Luke-Acts.* Minneapolis: Augsburg, 1981.

Talbert, C., ed. *Perspectives on Luke-Acts.* Mercer University, Macon, Ga.: National Association of Baptist Professors of Religion, 1978.

Tiede, D.L. *Prophecy and History in Luke-Acts.* Philadelphia: Fortress, 1980.

John

Barrett, C.K. *The Gospel according to St. John.* 2nd ed. Philadelphia: Westminster, 1978.

Culpepper, R.A. *Anatomy of the Fourth Gospel: A Study in Literary Design.* Philadelphia: Fortress, 1983.

Fortna, R.T. *The Gospel of Signs: A Reconstruction of the Narrative Source Underlying the Fourth Gospel.* New York: Cambridge University Press, 1970.

Kasemann, E. *The Testament of Jesus: A Study of the Gospel of John in the Light of Chapter 17.* Philadelphia: Fortress,, 1978.

Kysar, R. *John: The Maverick Gospel.* Atlanta: John Knox, 1976.

Martyn, J.L. *The Gospel of John in Christian History.* Mahwah, N.J.: Paulist Press, 1979.

Schein, B.E. *Following the Way: The Setting of John's Gospel.* Minneapolis: Augsburg, 1980.

Glossary

adoptionism an early church heresy which regarded Jesus as a good man gifted with divine power who was "adopted" by God as his son after the resurrection.

allegory a story in which each element has a hidden meaning; or a method of interpreting a story which ignores the literal meaning to give a second, secret meaning to every element in the story.

almah the Hebrew word meaning "a young woman of child-bearing age."

annotated Bible a contemporary translation of the Bible with critical notes, introductory articles, maps, and other aids to Bible study.

Antonia a fortress built by Herod the Great at the northwest corner of the temple enclosure in Jerusalem.

apocalypse, apocalyptic (from a Greek word meaning "revelation") a writing that expresses a world-view commonly held by both Jews and Christians in the first century A.D. that God was bringing the world to an end and beginning a new age. Such writings claim to reveal secret events which are leading up to the end of the present age and claim to predict the coming of a heavenly redeemer.

apocryphal gospel a gospel that is not included in the official list of New Testament books.

Aramaic a general term used to identify a group of similar Semitic dialects closely related to Hebrew, one of which was spoken in Palestine during the time of Jesus.

Ascension the final appearance of the risen Christ when he was "taken up into heaven" according to Luke's Easter story (see Luke 24:50-52 and Acts 1:6-11). Since the end of the fourth century the church has commemorated this event with a major feast on the fifth Thursday (the fortieth day) after Easter.

beatitudes sentences beginning with the word "Blessed" (in Greek, "happy") which introduce the Sermon on the Mount in Matthew (see Matthew 5:3-11 and compare Luke 6:17,20-23).

Beloved Disciple the anonymous follower of Jesus who is mentioned only in John's gospel where he is identified as the disciple whom Jesus loved (see 13:23-26, 19:25-27, 20:2-10, 21:20-23,24; see also 18:15-16 which mentions "another disciple" and the reference to an unnamed disciple of John the Baptist in 1:37-42). He is given a special place in John's gospel and may well have been the founder of the community for whom the gospel was written.

Benedictus the Latin translation of the first word of the Jewish-Christian hymn in Luke 1:68-79 which has become the central song of praise in the church's morning prayer.

Byzantine period in the history of the Middle East, the period of the imperial state church from the time of Constantine (313) until the Muslims took possession of Jerusalem (638).

Calvary see Golgotha

canon (from a Greek word meaning "rule" or "measure") the official list of books that make up the Bible.

canticle a song, other than the psalms, derived from the Bible which is used in the worship of the church.

chesed the Hebrew word meaning "responsible love."

Christ the Greek translation of the Hebrew word "Messiah" which means "the Anointed One." It is usually found with the definite article in the Greek text of the gospels ("the Christ"), which makes it clear that this is a title attributed to Jesus and originally not part of his name.

christology the branch of Christian theology that considers the person of Jesus, his humanity and divinity, and his role in the salvation of the world. A "high" christology is one that emphasizes the divinity of Jesus.

Church of the Holy Sepulchre the Crusader church built in Jerusalem over the site of Jesus' crucifixion and burial.

commentary a guide to the study of the Bible designed to explain the text and provide important introductory and background information.

concordance   a listing by book, chapter, and verse of every occurrence of every important word in the Bible. An analytical concordance separates these citations according to the various Hebrew or Greek words translated by each English word.

davar   the Hebrew term meaning "word."

decalogue   the "ten Words," a more precise name for the Ten Commandments (see Exodus 20:1).

Decapolis   the Ten Towns, a district in Palestine made up of a league of ten cities which lies southeast of Galilee and across the Jordan, east of Perea.

Diatesseron   the harmony of the four gospels produced by Tatian in the second century.

docetism, docetic   (from a Greek word meaning "to seem" or "to appear to be") an early church heresy which affirmed that Jesus was not truly human but only appeared to be.

emeth   the Hebrew word literally meaning "truth" but in the New Testament its Greek equivalent is often better translated "faithfulness" with the emphasis on the faithfulness of God.

Emmanuel   (the Hebrew name meaning "God-with-us") Matthew's particular name for Jesus taken from the prophecy in Isaiah 7:14.

End, the   see *eschaton*

Epiphany   (from a Greek word meaning "manifestation") an important Christian feast celebrated on January 6 (Twelfth Night). It originated in the church in the East in the third century where it celebrated the baptism of Jesus. In the West it has become associated with the visit of the Wise Men.

eschatology, eschatological   (see *eschaton)* a branch of theology concerned with the last things, that is, the end of the world, the Second Coming of the Messiah, the day of resurrection, the final judgment, and the beginning of the new age.

eschaton a Greek word meaning "the end," that is, the end of the world, the culmination and goal of history.

eucharist (from a Greek word meaning "thanksgiving") the principal act of worship of the Christian church: the liturgy in which the community becomes the body of the risen Christ by hearing his word and by knowing him "in the breaking of the bread."

evangelist a composer of a gospel, one who proclaims the good news that Jesus is Lord and the Christ.

Exile, the the period when the Israelites were expelled from their homeland (from the northern kingdom of Israel in 722 B.C. by the Assyrians and from the southern kingdom of Judah by 587 B.C. by the Babylonians) and forced to live in Mesopotamia until the decree of Cyrus the Persian in 538 B.C. permitted those who so desired to return.

Exodus, the the event in which God rescued the Israelites from slavery in Egypt, gave them the Torah through Moses, and led them to the promised land; the event celebrated at Passover.

form criticism an approach to the study of the Bible that examines the literary form and the situation in life of the individual units of material in the writings in order to reconstruct the history and development of the oral tradition which lies behind the writings.

formula citation the practice of introducing a quotation from the Old Testament with the phrase "to fulfill what the Lord has spoken by the prophet," which is particularly characteristic of Matthew.

Fourth Gospel the gospel according to John.

Galilee the territory north of Samaria under the rule of the tetrarch Herod Antipas during Jesus' ministry.

gentiles all non-Jewish peoples; the word comes from a Hebrew word for "nations".

gnosticism, gnostic (from a Greek word meaning "knowledge") a complex religious movement which took many forms. Characteristic of its teachings were the distinction between the "creator god" and the supreme, unknowable Divine Being, the belief that the created world was imperfect and evil, and the teaching that some persons had a divine spark in them that could be fanned by the right knowledge which would be brought by a divine redeemer. Salvation, therefore, was by this special knowledge that would enable the elect to escape the bondage of this evil creation and return to the Divine Being.

Golgotha (Calvary) a transliteration of the Aramaic word for "skull." It is the "place of a skull" where Jesus was crucified (see Mark 15:22, Matthew 27:33, John 19:17). In Luke 23:33 this site is identified by the Greek word for "skull," *kranion*. The Latin word used to translate this term in the Vulgate, the Latin version of the Bible, is *Calvaria*. This, in turn, has been transliterated in some English versions into the term "Calvary."

gospel the good news that Jesus is Lord and the Christ; a unique literary composition, probably invented by Mark, consisting of a proclamation in narrative form that Jesus is Lord and the Christ.

Gospel of Thomas a document discovered in 1945 as part of a library of ancient writings found at Nag Hammadi in Egypt. It contains a series of 114 sayings attributed to Jesus but no narrative, that is, no birth story, no miracle stories, no passion narrative, or account of the resurrection.

grace the generous love of God freely offered, through Jesus, to all who respond to him by faith.

Greek Version of the Old Testament commonly called the Septuagint: the translation of the Hebrew scriptures into Greek in the Hellenistic period for Greek-speaking Jews, plus some additional writings in Greek that did not occur in the Hebrew Bible. These were the scriptures used by the early Christians and quoted in the New Testament. In modern translations of the Old Testament the extra Greek writings are either included with the books of the Old Testament and classified as deutero-canonical (Roman

Catholic), or separated into another section of the Bible called the Apocrypha (Anglican), or omitted (Protestant).

Hanukkah   the mid-winter Jewish festival of eight days commemorating the reconsecration of the temple after the victory of the Maccabees over Antiochus Epiphanes, who had descrated the temple with an altar to Zeus.

Hebrew Bible   the scriptures considered authentic by the Jews since the first century A.D. consisting of twenty-four books written in Hebrew which are arranged in three sections: the Torah (Law), the Prophets, and the Writings.

Hellenistic   the period of history from the time of Alexander the Great (356-323 B.C.) to the first century A.D. as well as the Greek civilization and culture of that age.

Herodium   the hilltop fortress palace built by Herod the Great near Bethlehem. According to tradition Herod was buried here.

hokmah   the Hebrew word meaning "wisdom."

incarnate   (from a Latin word meaning "to become flesh") the theological term used to sum up the proclamation in John 1:14 that "the Word became flesh and dwelt among us."

Idumea, Idumean   the term used in the Greek Version of the Old Testament for Edom, a region south of Judea. The local rulers of Palestine in the Herodian dynasty were Idumeans.

Judaizers   Jewish Christians who believe it was first necessary to become a Jew before becoming a Christian; and, in a general sense, Jewish Christians who continued to practice and stress their Jewish tradition.

kiddush   the Jewish blessing, or sanctification, of the sabbath and holy days over a cup of wine.

law and the prophets   a reference to the two main sections of the Hebrew Bible: the Torah (law) and the Prophets.

literary criticism   an approach to the study of the Bible that seeks to discover the authors of the books of the Bible and the written sources they used. Recently more emphasis has been placed on the study of the literary nature of the writings and the relationship between story and meaning.

liturgy (from a Greed word meaning "work of the people") in Christian usage the term is used in two senses: 1) to designate all formal worship services of the church and 2) to designate specifically the eucharist, the principal worship service of the church.

Magnificat the Latin translation of the first word of the Jewish-Christian hymn in Luke 1:46-55 which has become the central song of praise in the church's evening prayer.

manna an edible substance that provided part of the food of the Israelites during their wilderness wanderings after the Exodus. It is the liquid honeydew secretion of two closely related scale insects, which dries in the desert sun into solid drops of a sticky sugar.

Masada Herod the Great's fortified place on the Western shore of the Dead Sea where after the fall of Jerusalem in A.D. 70 the Zealots held off the Tenth Roman Legion for a year before committing mass suicide rather than surrender.

Maundy Thursday the Thursday in Holy Week called the "Thursday of the Commandment" (Maundy) because, according to John's gospel, Jesus gave his disciples a new commandment after the Last Supper.

messianic secret a device of Mark to explain why Jesus was not recognized as the Messiah at the beginning of his ministry. According to Mark, only the demons recognize who Jesus is until he is ready to go to Jerusalem for the final week of his ministry.

Migdal Eder the Hebrew title "Tower of the Flock," which was first attributed to Jerusalem and then assigned to Bethlehem.

miracle a sign of God's presence in the world that evokes awe and wonder.

Mishnah the oral interpretation of Torah, codified in about A.D. 200, which became the basis of the Talmud.

mitzvot the Hebrew word meaning "commandments."

Nativity the feast celebrating the birth of Jesus which is observed on December 25 and is the focus of the Christmas celebration in the church in the West.

Nazarite   a sacred person who marks his vow of self-dedication to God by letting his hair grow and abstaining from wine and strong drink.

Neo-Platonism   the philosophical system of Plotinus and his successors. It drew its ideas from Plato but its purpose was more religious. It taught that the Absolute, which could only be known by a method of abstraction, could be reached by mystical experience.

netzer   the Hebrew word meaning "branch."

Nicene Creed   the formula of the church's faith issued by the Council of Constantinople in 381. It is an expansion of the creed issued in 325 by the Council of Nicaea (from which it takes its name) which, in turn, had its origin in the baptismal creed of Jerusalem.

Nunc Dimittis   the Latin translation of the opening words of the Jewish-Christian hymn in Luke 2:29-32, which is traditionally used at the late evening service of compline.

parable   a story based on everyday experience used to illustrate a point or illuminate a teaching.

paradigm   a model.

parallel version of the gospels   an edition of the text of the Synoptic gospels, or all four gospels, arranged in columns for convenience in comparing common material.

Parousia   the Greek term for the Second Coming of the risen Christ.

parthenos   the Greek word meaning "virgin."

passion narrative   the account of the arrest, trial, and crucifixion of Jesus in each of the four gospels.

Perea   a territory just east of the Jordan river and the Dead Sea from Samaria and Judea which was under the rule of Herod Antipas of Galilee during Jesus' ministry.

pericope   a distinct unit of material which is a basic component of a gospel.

Pharisees   one of the major sects of Judaism in the first century A.D. and the only one which survived the destruction of the temple in the year 70. They were careful interpreters of the Torah, which they held in high esteem, and at the same time they were open to new religious ideas such as belief in resurrection.

praetorium the official residence of a provincial Roman governor or procurator. In Jerusalem in Jesus' time the praetorium was the Citadel, the upper palace built by Herod the Great by the Joppa Gate.

Prophets, the the second section of the Hebrew Bible which contains the books of the "former prophets"—Joshua, Judges, 1 and 2 Samuel, 1 and 2 Kings—as well as the prophetic scrolls of Isaiah, Jeremiah, Ezekiel, and The Book of the Twelve.

Q a hypothetical source used by Matthew and Luke composed of a collection of sayings attributed to Jesus, arranged in a topical order, which are primarily eschatological in tone. Scholars named this sayings source "Q," the first letter of the German word for "source."

redaction criticism an approach to the study of the Bible which takes seriously the creative work of the composer of each book, and, for each of the gospels, seeks to understand the evangelist's theological outlook and the type of congregation for whom he composed his gospel.

Samaritans people who lived in the territory between Galilee and Judea. In New Testament times they were despised by the Jews. Originally they were Israelites who separated from their countrymen after the northern kingdom fell to the Assyrians in 722 B.C. Their Bible consists of the five books of the Torah, and they built their temple on Mount Gerizim.

Sanhedrin the supreme Jewish council of seventy-one members during post-exilic times in Jerusalem. Under Herod the Great and then under the Romans its authority was curtailed, and after the Jewish revolt in A.D. 70 it ceased to exist.

Second Coming the term used to translate *Parousia,* the future coming again of the risen Christ.

seder (a Hebrew word meaning "order") the order of the

family service on Passover at which the story of the Exodus is told and the event celebrated.

Semitic pertaining to the peoples speaking one of the family of languages which includes Aramaic, Hebrew, and Arabic, and to their culture. In the ancient world these people occupied an area stretching from northern Arabia all the way north to Turkey and east to Iraq.

shekinah the Hebrew name for God, dwelling within his world, resting in the midst of the people.

sitz im leben a German phrase which means "situation in life." In the study of the gospels it is used to identify the situation in which Jesus used a saying or a story and the situation in which the same passage was used in the early church.

Son of God a title used in the Old Testament to denote a divine being and in the New Testament, particularly in the gospels, to refer to Jesus, a title which emphasizes his unique relationship to God.

Son of man a title given by the Jews to the apocalyptic redeemer who will come at the end of the age. By the time the gospels were written the church had applied the title to Jesus.

Stocism a school of Greek philosophy founded by Zeno in the fourth century B.C., which became the dominant philosophy of the Hellenistic world and then the Roman Empire. The fundamental teaching is that virtue is the only good and vice the only evil. The wise person, therefore, will be indifferent to pleasure and pain, wealth and poverty, success and misfortune. The Stoic seeks to make his will one with the purpose that governs the universe.

Succoth the Jewish autumn festival of thanksgiving for the blessing of the harvest and God's protection.

Suffering Servant the anonymous prophetic figure described in the songs in Isaiah 42:1-4, 49:1-6, 50:4-11, and especially in 52:13-53:12 where he is portrayed as the innocent man who goes silently and willingly to his death, giving his life for the guilty.

synoptic the adjective used to designate the interdependence of the first three gospels—Matthew, Mark, and Luke—which have a common perspective (which see "with the same eye").

Talmud the collection of rabbinic interpretations of the Torah consisting of the Mishnah and the Gemara which was completed about A.D. 500.

tetrarchy a fourth part of an area under the rule of a tetrarch, a title that can also mean simply "a petty ruler." During the ministry of Jesus, Herod Antipas was tetrarch of Galilee.

Torah a Hebrew word meaning "instruction." Specifically, the Torah is the first five books of the Hebrew Bible: Genesis, Exodus, Leviticus, Numbers, and Deuteronomy. In a wider sense it includes the entire Hebrew Bible, and in the broadest sense it signifies both the written and oral instructions by which Jews govern their lives.

Tower of the Flock see *Migdal Eder*

truth see *emeth*

Via Dolorosa the Latin phrase meaning "The Way (or Road) of Sorrows." It is the name given to the route which pilgrims since the thirteenth century believe Jesus took when he carried his cross from the Antonia through the streets of Jerusalem to Golgotha (the Church of the Holy, Sepulchre today). Historically, the route led in the opposite direction from the Citadel by the Joppa Gate to Golgotha.

virgin birth the teaching more precisely called the virginal conception, based on Matthew 1:18-25 and Luke 1:26-38, which proclaims that Jesus became the Son of God by the power of the Holy Spirit, not at the resurrection nor at his baptism, but at his birth.

Wisdom with a capital "W," is the personification of wisdom and described in the Old Testament Wisdom literature as existing with God from the beginning and descending from heaven to dwell with humankind.

word the English translation of the Greek *logos,* the masculine counterpart of the feminine Greek *sophia* (Hebrew *hokmah)* which means "Wisdom."

Writings, the   the third section of the Hebrew scriptures along with the Torah and the Prophets.

Yahweh   the scholars' reconstruction of the Hebrew proper name of God. Pious Jews do not pronounce the name out of reverence, but say in its place the Hebrew word for "Lord." So some modern English translations render this word "Lord." Others translate it "Jehovah," and a few versions use the scholars' reconstruction of the name, "Yahweh."

About the Author

R. Rhys Williams is a retired Episcopal priest now living in Nova Scotia with his wife, Mary. He is Professor Emeritus of Marist College in Poughkeepsie, New York. In addition to his 17 years at Marist, Dr. Williams has also taught and been involved in campus ministry at Nashotah House in Wisconsin, The General Theological Seminary, New York, and was twice Visiting Professor at St. George's College in Jerusalem (1974 and 1982). Dr. Williams earned Master of Divinity and Doctor of Theology degrees from The General Theological Seminary, as well as a Masters in Semitic Languages from Columbia University. His pastoral experience spans 40 years and includes serving as Rector of St. Peter's Church and Christ Church in Millbrook and Poughkeepsie, New York, respectively, and of SS. Mary and Jude Church in Northeast Harbor, Maine. He was curate at St. Mark's Church in New Canaan, Connecticut, and at the Church of the Holy Spirit, Lake Forest, Illinois.